The
Yankee Professor's
Guide To
Life in Nova Scotia

Being an Account of a Year in an
Expatriate's Life, Touching on Matters
Leading to the Realization that
Nova Scotia Is Exactly the Right Place to
Thwart Distracting Ambition,
Teach What You Know,
Keep Bees,
Understand the Outdoors and the
Self in the Outdoors,
Cherish Friendship, Write as Best You Can,
Love Those You're Privileged To Live With,
and
Serve God as Necessity Imposes

The Yankee Professor's Guide To
Life in Nova Scotia

*Being an Account of a Year in an
Expatriate's Life, Touching on Matters
Leading to the Realization that
Nova Scotia Is Exactly the Right Place to
Thwart Distracting Ambition,
Teach What You Know,
Keep Bees,
Understand the Outdoors and the
Self in the Outdoors,
Cherish Friendship, Write as Best You Can,
Love Those You're Privileged To Live With,
and
Serve God as Necessity Imposes*

By Philip Milner

LANCELOT PRESS
Hantsport, Nova Scotia

Book and cover design and layout by Michele Pittman.

The cover painting, *Sarah and Ed's House*, is used with
the permission of its owners, Sarah and Ed Carty,
and the painter, Anna Syperek.

Parts of this book appeared in very different form in
*The Fiddlehead, The Globe and Mail, Peter Gzowski's New
Morningside Papers, Quarry, The Chicago Sun-Times
Magazine, Notre Dame Magazine*, pseudonymously in the
Reporter, and elsewhere.

LANCELOT PRESS LIMITED, Hantsport, Nova Scotia.
Office and production facilities situated on Highway No. 1,
1/2 mile east of Hantsport.

MAILING ADDRESS:
P.O. Box 425, Hantsport, N.S. B0P 1P0

ACKNOWLEDGEMENT: This book has been published
with the assistance of the Canada Council.

"... if you'll let a guide direct you
   Who only has at heart your getting lost ..."

— *Robert Frost,* **Directive**

A character is either real or imaginary? If you think that, *hypocrite lecteur,* I can only smile. You do not even think of your own past as quite real; you dress it up, you gild it or blacken it, censor it, tinker with it... fictionalize it, in a word, put it away on a shelf — your book, your romanced autobiography. We are all in flight from real reality. That is the basic definition of *Homo sapiens.*

— *John Fowles,* **French Lieutenant's Woman**

*For Marilyn, who helped with the real parts
and put up with the rest.*

Contents

1   Home If Not Native Land

This hour I tell things in confidence,
I might not tell everybody, but I will tell you.
— *Walt Whitman*

There are two stoplights in the 2000-kilometre stretch
of Trans-Canada highway between Sydney, Cape Breton,
and Windsor, Ontario. I could see them both from my
office in the high rise.

"How do you get from Vancouver to Antigonish?" is
a riddle Antigonishers like to ask those from away.
Answer: you head east on the Trans-Canada and turn left
at the first stoplight.

As far as I know that is true. Forcing the
transportation system to yield on its principle of limited
access in order to boost the commerce of one town of
5,000 people is testimony to our ability to choose
politicians in Antigonish. So is the presence of the
Philatelic Centre, that upper-Canadian glass and brick
structure with its landscaped grounds and mercury vapour
lights. It appeared on St. Ninian Street, a block east of the
Cathedral, shortly before the '84 federal election. The
wharves in the fishing villages of Antigonish County are as
fine as anyone's. Many of them were also rebuilt shortly
before the winds of governmental reform blew the Liberals
out of power, and our legendary MP, the Honourable Allen
J. MacEachen, into the Senate.

I spend a lot of time looking out that window. Today,
I see pulp trucks edging through the mist with their lights

on. Seagulls and big crows huddle on the football field. A couple of times a week a long black Cadillac carries someone I knew or knew about up the hill to the graveyard on the other side of the Trans-Canada where, as we say, my own remains will one day rest. At night, the headlights reflect off the headstones, like vigil lights flickering.

"I looked at that highway and that cemetery almost every day for five years," a thoughtful historian said, once, as we looked down from the sixth floor window, styrofoam coffee cups in hand. "One day it dawned on me that there are two ways out of Antigonish, and I was looking at them both."

Many of my younger colleagues turn inward in about their fifth year, the year they are awarded tenure. They don't say anything, but I know what they are thinking. It's not success at last.

"For this I watched the academic vice president read his mail out loud at coffee, suffered fools as a matter of course. For this I connived. My luck, ambition, and cunning brought me here and no farther."

They look appraisingly at us, their senior colleagues. They look at tiny Al the historian who spends his summers running a Bed and Breakfast, at the dean of arts with his mischievous grin and vile jokes. They look at Michael Stubbs, who celebrates his personal history as though he were Dante and Antigonish the Holy City, at me, I assume, with the obsessions I chronicle in these pages, and others they've noticed, no doubt, that I've not been honest enough to face. Will they end up as quirky and irrelevant as we are?

Whom the Gods would turn sour, they first award tenure.

"Halifax isn't the end of the world, but you can see it from there," a Montreal Canadian hockey player said when he was farmed out to Halifax for seasoning. What would he have said if they'd sent him to Antigonish?

Most of us are Catholic, and we are protected from ourselves by the Catholic Church and the watchful eyes of our neighbours. We attend St. Ninian's Cathedral, where masses are celebrated with Keltic sternness; or we attend the University Chapel, where masses tend to be long on loose good feeling. The president of St. Francis Xavier University, until last year, has always been a priest.

The question an outsider is asked most often in his first years in town is this: "And how do you like living in Antigonish?" Speaking as a survivor, I can tell you that the question has a correct answer: "I love it."

After tenure, some of us come out of the closet, admit to doubts about the idea of a Catholic university, the status of Antigonish as a model and beacon of hope to the third world, wonder if people elsewhere don't have just as much salt of the earth in them as people here do.

But there is only so much pleasure to be extracted from self-flagellation over one's unlucky stars. Many of us embrace Antigonish's slow rhythms, raise our kids, and cherish our quiet lives.

From the windows on the other side of the high rise, I look across at the spires of St. Ninian's Cathedral, at Braemore Elementary School, downtown Antigonish. Beyond that, Sugarloaf Mountain broods. It is grey in winter, green in summer. During spring and autumn, it turns a different colour every day.

The town hall is in an old brick building at the corner of Main and College Streets. The clock in the tower did not work for years. Five years ago, a friend of mine fixed it. On the sidewalk in front of the town hall there is a lovely sculpture of a huge horse being led by a woman. Her Scottish husband, wearing a tam, pushes the plough behind her. It was put there two years ago, just before Antigonish's centennial.

"Antigonish is a one-horse town," His Worship, Mayor Colin Chisholm, now says in speeches, and that is the horse he is talking about. On summer days, old people sit on the wooden bench beneath the horse; young cigarette-smokers gather in the early evening; drunks and lovers late at night.

The Pictou-Antigonish Regional Library uses the side door of the town hall. It has hissing radiators, a clean washroom, one large room bulging with books. Mrs. MacKinnon never fines you more than half a dollar, and she can tell you something helpful about each book on her shelves.

Through the library's distorting plate glass window, you can see the office of the *Casket*, our weekly newspaper. The *Casket* tells us what's on sale and says nice things or nothing at all about us. It is hard to imagine anyone raising a family in Antigonish without it.

The Triangle Tavern ("Grease and grog," as students say), up the street and across from the IGA, serves cold draught beer and salty pork chops. Town and gown meet there, often acrimoniously. At the Cottage Store and Restaurant ("The Gag"), you can eat the Motherlode Special, sit under one of the mounted deer heads, and tell your story to Betty, who will add a detail you didn't know. We have three banks, a credit union, four clothing stores, two Mets, Sears and MacIntosh's Hardware, and three taxi stands. The Five to a Dollar burned down. When it was re-built, the owner mounted a huge golden phoenix bird over the door. It was designed by a faculty husband who has since departed.

The franchises all came to town after I did. We might be the smallest town anywhere that has a Kentucky Fried, two Tim Horton's, a McDonald's, a Dairy Queen, and a Pizza Delight. The liquor commission is in the mall, a sprawling windowless building with an asphalt parking lot. If, driving by on the Trans-Canada, someone were to tell you it was a provincial prison, you would believe them. On Sundays, when the liquor commission is closed, the Moonlight Restaurant, at Main and Church, fills with solitary male diners wearing ball caps.

From a booth in front of its huge plate glass window, you can see three realtors, a sporting goods store, the United Church, the Bank of Commerce, and the busiest of our three stoplights.

We stop our cars on Main Street to let people out of parking lots. We invite people to turn left in front of us. There are three occasions for traffic snarls in Antigonish: after masses at the Cathedral; after hockey games at the arena; and, in summer, when a tourist's Winnebago has difficulty making the tight left turn at the light into Whidden's trailer court. If you hear a horn, you assume a teenaged driver is greeting a friend. That, or a tourist honked it. Our drivers are the politest I have ever seen. I did not know what "polite to a fault" meant until I came to live in Antigonish. It is easy to forget that politeness is a virtue when you are stuck behind someone who decides to let the traffic from church go ahead of him (and you!).

On summer evenings, the pleasant whir of chain saws

will be heard until dark. Sloppy piles of eight foot lengths become orderly stacks of blocked and split wood. In August and September, your own and your neighbours's kids carry cured firewood into basements. In October, smoke rises from most chimneys. There is an Antigonish smell, and I like it. Wood smoke mostly.

"How you going to get your wood?" we ask each other on these July days. And we stay for the most elaborate answer.

By April, we have burns on our hands and persistent coughs. We are tired of loading wood stoves. The burns heal quickly when we stop feeding the stoves; the coughs pass.

The United Church is at the stoplight on Main and Church Streets; the Anglicans gather at a grey and red chapel up the street beside the funeral home, and the Baptists are wedged between the Highland Trailer Court and the Trans-Canada. There are two Mormon missionaries in town. Their faces change, but you know them by their youth, their white shirts and ties, and their cheery good manners. If you let them into your house, they give you a pamphlet, tell you about Joe Smith, and say a prayer for you. It is not a bad deal, though Father MacLeod once gave a Sunday homily insisting we bar our doors to them.

2

My involvement with my neighbours in wood getting, church, gardening, squash, and raising kids makes me feel closer to people here than I have felt to people anywhere I have lived.

I do not want to exaggerate this closeness. My forays into what my non-professorly neighbours call the real world have not been particularly successful. It seemed unfair to my neighbours and to me that curb and gutter be provided to the newer houses at the top of our street and not to our equally deserving older farmhouses at the bottom. Because I was a professor, and eloquence is my business, I became the designated spokesperson for the six houses at the bottom of the street.

"Should we call you Doctor Milner or Professor Milner or Mr. Milner?" the mayor asked, lest his colleagues miss the lesson of my accent.

"It doesn't matter what you call me," I answered. "The town has installed curb and gutter at the top of the road, but not at the bottom. We need it worse at the bottom, because that is where the road floods in the spring."

The mayor nodded several times, then turned his eyes across the room to the door way. His shirt was white, his face and suit were grey, as were his huge eyebrows. In fact, the most colourful thing about him was his tie, a quiet Chisholm plaid.

"That'd be in the old MacLean house...," he said. "I know that house very well. I used to play in there when I was young. This'd be long before your time... er...

doctor... Professor..." He looked down at a piece of paper on his desk. "Milner. So..." he said, and he looked long at me, the professor who lived in the MacLean house.

"It seems unreasonable," I said. "If you put water and sewage service up there at the top of the hill, then it should logically go to the houses at the bottom, too."

The mayor turned his head away from the table, focused his eyes above the heads of his colleagues, toward something or someone standing outside the door.

"We don't think it's right," I added. "We brought photographs. These show what's going on."

Everyone except Mayor Chisholm watched me remove the eight by ten black and white photos from the manila envelope. No one spoke while the councillors thumbed through the pictures of overflowing drainage ditches, which were slowly passed up the table to the mayor, who examined each one, and then piled them beside his ash tray.

"These are good photographs," he said. "Trouble is, they show what I already know."

"We just want you to know what we know," I said.

"Well, you succeeded there," the mayor said.

"We want you to know the *truth*," I added.

The mayor smiled his tired smile.

"I know a few things," he said. "Not as much as some people..."

He lowered his eyes to my face for a second, and raised a hand.

"I know, I know," he said.

He tapped a Players from his pack, and lit it. A cloud of smoke engulfed him and the councillors at his end of the table. He began to speak. He spoke for ten minutes, never looking at me, occasionally moving his eyes from the doorway to look at a fellow councillor, all of whom seemed to be nodding affirmatively to the rhythms of his speech.

Though I'd thought my little speech had focused the debate on the logic of providing the bottom of our road with water and sewage service like that which the top of the street had received, I was wrong. The mayor decided that what I really needed was a lesson in Antigonish history.

Antigonish history, it turned out, was a long slow quest for curb and gutter. The mayor remembered "steam shovels," the intransigence of the provincial politicians, the men digging in the muddy streets with short-handled shovels in the days before asphalt, the upityness of the professors even then, the stolid determination of the council to provide everyone in town — Grit and PC, rich and poor, professor and pulp cutter — with water and sewage services as quickly and as cheaply as was humanly possible.

"Times are changing, and people forget. It needs to be written down, and fortunately, someone's writing it all down, one of your ..." Here he stopped, and searched his mind for exactly the right word. "One of your ... Colleagues!" he proclaimed. "Up there at the university ... Dr. Pat Walsh. I hope Dr. Walsh puts a chapter in his book about water and sewage service. It's an interesting story, and its worth a chapter of any history of this town. Dr. Walsh's a hard worker; and, of course, a very ambitious man."

His Worship continued. People in Antigonish began working for water and sewage service when the university only had four hundred students, when the professors were all priests. In fact the fathers of some of the councillors in the very room we were sitting in had been instrumental in introducing curb and gutter to the town, on a small scale. of course, but, given the poverty of the town and eastern Nova Scotia in general, that was the best that could be done.   Now, it's being extended to the near county residents, who don't even pay town taxes, but who, nonetheless, don't seem to be a bit shy about giving advice.

"Not a bit shy about that," he repeated, his eyes far away, above the door ledge, his mind on something more pressing than my petition.

He turned his eyes toward me for a moment, and I saw pain in his soft brown eyes. Again, he raised his hand defensively.

"I know, I know..." he said.   "Frankly, Doctor..., university professors weren't much interested in town improvements in those days."

"We only want what is reasonable," I said.

I glared. Let my righteous silence fill the room.

"That, too," he said sadly. "Eastern Nova Scotia is very poor. People here used to be patient, used to wait for things." He looked at me. "But times change. I know the Council is happy to see so many professors interested in the town now, ... er, Doctor. . . er, Professor... ." He looked down at his yellow pad. "Professor Milner! ... I want to assure you that you'll get curb and gutter out there as soon as we can possibly do it. Does that sound fair enough?"

"We'll be watching," I said.

The mayor shook his head.

3

Canada's third national political party belongs, by default, to the St. Francis Xavier University faculty. One or another of my colleagues runs for MP or MLA in almost every election. He gets his picture in the *Casket* wearing a pin-striped suit. He appears on the ATV Evening News, saying the things that he has been saying for years in the coffee room. He asks us for votes and tax deductible donations. He seems to convince himself he is going to win. He gets 14% of the vote.

I had my taste of politics. I was president of the faculty association. Wearing a modest blue tie with a subdued red diamond pattern and a quiet dark blue suit, I waxed knowledgeably about librarian's benefits, pension plans, the right to appeal, equities and inequities. Fighting heroically for a more reasonable Faculty Salary Scale, I became one who counted. You would find me at parties pressed against the refrigerator by supplicants. I visited the great cities of North America, stayed in luxury hotels, ate in gourmet restaurants. My greatest trick: I learned that if you made university administrators admit something was "unreasonable," they had to change it.

I became president of the Writer's Federation of Nova Scotia too, became a key player on the Nova Scotia Confederation of University Faculty Associations. It became not uncommon for me to be huddled up with cabinet ministers and deputy premiers in my fights for Nova Scotian writers and university faculty. I fell into whatever posture the situation called for, gladly wrote what was needed. I was the man for the job. The Man for the

Job. The AVP and the Deans and the EVP and I drank together.

I returned late from Ottawa or Halifax or Toronto tired and anxious, but full of my accomplishments, at least on one level. Even as I was making the speeches, chairing meetings, stroking my constituents, hurrying to Ottawa for important meetings, I found thoughts I didn't want popping into my head. I tried to fight down the suspicion that the drum I was pounding was full of air; worse, that I was full of air. What if the life I was leading was the wrong one? What if I'd made a wrong turn? One day I realized I had become the kind of person I did not particularly like.

On F. Scott Fitzgerald's principle that, if you don't get what you like, you'd better learn to like what you get, I finished my term as president of the faculty association, and refused another term. I gave up my office in Nicholson Hall, and moved to the basement of a building that housed the university kitchen and the Sisters of St. Martha. My wife and I moved from Viewville Street, and bought a ramshackle house on the edge of town.

A true Maritimer would accept some things I question, not notice some things that I love, know the importance of some things I don't even see. I don't know exactly what a "true Maritimer" is, but I know that a person who spent the first thirty years of his or her life in Indiana will never be one.

But if you live here long enough, you're not an American either. I went back to the American midwest for the Head Family Reunion. A hundred Heads were there in splendid red t-shirts with Head Family Reunion in big letters. The reunion took place at my cousin Curby's farm, near Mt. Victory, a place so deep in the boondocks that the nearest motel was 25 miles away. A pig roast, a hay ride, a quiet so deep it was joy to go to bed at night. We hugged and marvelled at how long it had been since we'd seen cousins and aunts we cared a lot about once, drank beer (surreptiously; a fault lines runs through my family over alcohol), ate corn-on-the-cob (I'd forgotten how much I missed American midwestern corn-on-the-cob), and had a talent show. We put names on old photos, marvelled how slim some of us looked, how chubby most of us had become.

It was the talent show that made me realize I am no longer an American. There was a cute little joke told by my cute four year old third cousin. Then, two more third cousins worked the hula hoops. Then a truly talented third or fourth cousin (I'd never heard her last name before) sang "Try to Remember" so thrillingly, so perfectly, that I would not be surprised if she becomes a famous opera singer. There followed a corny skit in which thirty of my relatives, including me, were drafted into going down front and doing dumb things. Then, two more third cousins juggled eggs (they broke!) and did the hula hoop at the same time. All of this, of course, was as funny and no more strained than some of the things on America's Funniest Home Videos.

Then, my third cousin, so pert and winning that my mother said that she looked like the young Mary Tyler Moore, stood and spoke into a microphone, attached to a boom box.

"I'd like you to sing along," she said, "but first let's listen to the song we're going to sing along with." She pushed a button on the box. Guitar strains and the gravelly down home voice of Lee Greenwood filled the air. He sang a song about how great Detroit cars are, how beautiful the Tennessee hills are, how blue the Pacific, how majestic the fields of growing golden grain, how Americans will go to any length to help less fortunate people become free.

While the song played, my cousin passed out American flags. The staffs were toothpicks, the flags couldn't have been an inch and a half long. We were each given one.

My cousin wore a red, white and blue American flag-inspired skirt, with a white blouse and a red and white and blue vest. On her head she wore a red, white and blue panama hat with stars on it.

Then, she told us to stand and sing along. We stood, a hundred of us, waved our tiny American flags, and sang along with Lee Greenwood. When my relatives waved their American flags, cheered, and sang that patriotic American song, I came as close to an authentic Canadian emotion as someone from Indiana can come. I felt a slightly smug sense of quiet superiority to the proceedings of my rambunctious American cousins, a feeling all the more Canadian for the fact that I didn't want anyone except my wife and kids to know I was feeling it.

Then we carried our folding chairs around behind the barn for the fireworks show. We watched a fireworks show that was at least as expensive and elaborate at the one that the Canadian government foots the bill for on Canada Day at Columbus Field in Antigonish.

"You must have spent a fortune on the fireworks," was all I said to one of my second or third cousins.

Which, of course, was seen as a compliment.

"It was worth it," my cousin answered proudly. "For this family! For the Fourth of July."

I met cousins who were opposed to Bush and for him, against the Iraq war and for it, socialists and capitalists: my family ran the gamut, but all (except me and my wife and kids) seemed to believe that being an American is a very important and precious thing.

An American tends to think that loving his or her country will make a difference. An American tends to think that he or she will arrive at the Golden Gate one day, and show St. Peter an American flag lapel pin, and tell St. Peter than he or she has always been a loyal American who stood for the national anthem and would die for the U.S.A. if necessary, that this will make a difference.

4

By now I have lived much more than half my adult life in Canada. Still, when asked if I'm an American, I say yes, I'm an American, and unless the conversation goes on for a while, I do not add that I am a Canadian citizen. I've learned that Canadians, when they ask, are not asking about citizenship.

That part of me that is American is not mine to give up or a citizenship court's to change. My accent, my directness, my political assumptions, my reflex sneer at mention of the Queen. I'm a hybrid. My writing style mixes Indiana shit-kicker and Maritime diffidence. My accent is the metaphor. It takes on more of a Scottish lilt every day, becomes a little politer and less assertive every time I notice a change. I cannot speak five words without pronouncing one of them in a slightly different way that I learned in Indiana.

Still, I wish to assign that part of me that is mine to assign, to this place. My family, my vocation, most of my friends, and more and more of my past are here. My life is here, but if I don't let the Indiana twang in, I hear affectation in every syllable I speak or write.

Jiggs, our mostly beagle, chases every car that comes down our fork. "Don't worry!" I shout at the cars he manages to stop. "He won't bite!," I say, Eeee-own-BUY! as I've heard my neighbour say it. My kids speak with that Scottish lilt that used to sound quaint to my ear. With what help I commandeer from them and their friends, I will cut and split and stack ten cords of fire wood before this month is over. I know more about purple thrushes, barn swallows, pileated woodpeckers, and rose-breasted grosbeaks than I imagined there was to know, and I learned most of it here.

I came to Antigonish, Nova Scotia, for money, respect, and to escape a seventeen hour work day. Laws have since been passed to prevent American professors like me from coming. We took jobs away from real Canadians.

Certainly, anybody who comes to a foreign country on the near edge of middle-age is, in some sense, damaged merchandise. I am Canadian enough not to be depressed by these laws, though I watch my new colleagues, native Canadians all, young men and women who do not seem to marry or raise children or keep gardens, who sneer at the brands of wine available at the Antigonish liquor commission, while giving all to our profession and its airless politics. I hope Canada is getting a good deal.

I had never been east of Pittsburgh or nearer to Canada than Pontiac, Michigan, when I came here. Canada suggested good fishing, nice people, snow, and this phrase from my high school geography book: CANADA, THE SLEEPING GIANT. I didn't come to wake Canada up nor to take it over. I came here to live a life. That, for me, entails raising my kids, teaching as well as I can, and writing as truthfully as I can.

I am aware of a form of Maritime writing by others who come here from some place else. Could there be a surer way of proving your non-Maritimeness than a speech like this?

"I coached four little league teams, went on CBC forty-seven times telling how great the Maritimes are and how much I love it here. I have lived here twenty years. I love the ocean, the Bell Museum, Joseph Howe's memory, salted cod, and the smell of the sea. I wrote three books and forty-seven essays that tell how wonderful the Maritimes are."

"And Maritimers are the best damned people in the world, the salt of the earth. I love them all. I love their down-to-earth ways, their humility. I have been invited to live in Toronto, Paris, London, and New York. I could go any place, and they'd be glad to pay me big bucks. Offers come over the phone from everywhere, but here I am. So why don't you acknowledge that I am one of you?"

Loving the place or the people or the pace of life has nothing to do with it. Is there a surer way of demonstrating that you are an outsider? I'm not saying that Maritimers have smaller egos than Ontarians or Americans (Not for a second!), but I am saying that people formed here are much less likely to let themselves get away with such visible self-celebration, less likely to fall into certain forms of affectation. Their mothers wouldn't stand for it. Their cousins and second cousins and the people they grew up with would laugh.

Those of us from away are not Maritimers because of what we carry with us. If you grew up in Indiana, as I did, you carry the rhythms of that place in your assumptions, in your accent (an apt metaphor), in the way you walk, even. When I look at the old rusting anchor on the edge of the sea, I feel associations and the lack of associations I picked up elsewhere.

When I hear someone shouting his undying love for this place and its people (always in an accent as alien as my own), and wondering why they don't know how much he (always a he) cares, I head for the door.

Sometimes, I wish it was me that Alistair Graham or Bill Gillis or Mayor Chisholm or the legendary Allen J. MacEachen turned to at 3:00 a.m. when the party is over, and the people they had to be nice to have gone home, and the last bottle of rum is being opened among the intimates. Sometimes I think I'd like to be the kind of person who is in that room with the real locals.

But not often. I carry a charge of loneliness for an Indiana town that now exists only in my mind (and my wife's mind). I was an insider there. I remember my parents, who were sure that they lived in the only place in the world where people were fully human, the only place where friends were true. I remind myself that I gave up my insider status to live in a place where I am free from knowing what my neighbours are thinking about me, free to make up my own mind about who I like or trust partly because I don't know who the good families in town are, free to be surprised by the quiet rhythms of my neighbours's lives, and by the originality of the truths that pop into my head, and then into my writing.

It is my sad duty to report that those Americans, and Ontarians and others who tell you that the Maritimes is the best place in the world and that Maritimers are the best people in the world are not telling the truth. That they are kidding themselves first makes it only a little forgivable.

In the pages that follow I will tell you what I see. After half a lifetime, I can't go back. My accent is more foreign in Indiana than it is here.

Nationalists notwithstanding, a Canadian is not by definition a person born here. I have tried to tell, in these pages, what I've learned living most of my adult life in Antigonish, Nova Scotia.

You can hardly walk three miles in Antigonish County without finding a well, a stone foundation, a ramshackle fence, an orchard with apple trees forty feet high, suckers shooting up everywhere. In September those trees bend with clusters of apples smaller than golf balls. In February the bare black branches rise above the snowy fields and skewed fences. The apples from these trees taste like no others. Some leave an aftertaste as though they'd been dipped in alum. Others surprise you with their delicacy. The worst of them can be pressed. The juice is delicious and good for you, but you won't want to get far from home for a couple hours after drinking it.

The rocky soil, the salt wind off the Atlantic, the short growing season, and the long winter conspire to twist the trees and apples into odd shapes.   You can learn to like these blighted and gnarled apples.   If you do, and you find yourself some place where they have only the flawless round apples produced for big city consumers, you miss them.

2 Statues, cairns, sculptures, monuments

Old paint on canvas, as it ages, sometimes becomes transparent. When that happens it is possible, in some pictures, to see the original lines: a tree will show through a woman's dress, a child makes way for a dog, a large boat is no longer on an open sea. That is called pentimento because the painter "repented," changed his mind. Perhaps it would be as well as to say that the old conception, replaced by a later choice, is a way of seeing and then seeing again.

- Lillian Hellman, *Pentimento*

For a long time I felt Antigonishers were humbler than other people. Nice people who don't boast, and who make few claims for themselves. But the town itself, I discovered, is felt by its citizens to be a small miracle. And Antigonishers are special people because they and their parents and their parents have lived their lives in this special place. They are so aware of their specialness that they never need to shout it. Antigonish has, after all, given the world several bishops, Bruce MacKinnon's cartoons, the Antigonish Movement, Paul MacLean of the St. Louis Blues, more than its share of Senators and MPs, and the *Casket*.

You will know us by what we show you and what you gather from what we tell you. Can anyone, on an August day, look at Antigonish and not see these things, put here by Antigonishers to tell themselves and those who bother to look exactly who they are? Like Antigonishers themselves, the lapidary art does not shout. Still, perhaps no town this side of medieval Byzantium has erected so much to define itself.

I speak of the Cenotaph that was built to commemorate Antigonish's role in the first world war; the new statue of the Scottish settlers in front of the town hall; the cairns, those mysterious piles of stone and cement with coats-of-arms that proclaim the presence among us of the Chisholms and the MacDougalls and the invisible Chattan clan; the steel sculptures of protesting humanity made of what looks like old auto transmissions in front of and beside the post office, and, my favourite, the statue of the old bishop across from the cairns on St. Ninian and West Street at the university's one way street.

Antigonishers walk past them, sit under them, answer questions about them if they can, but live in the shadow of the history they proclaim.

2

The Old Bishop should be called the Unknown Bishop. The greenish-silver letters that once proclaimed his name and accomplishments, are almost all worn away. There's an N on one side of the base, some pieces of lead which once must have been letters, on another. Some say it's Bishop Cameron, others that it's Bishop MacKinnon.

Who ever it is, he is there, always, erect and white as snow, his cape buttoned from his neck to the tops of his shoes, breviary in hand. He doesn't look over the town, eyes raised toward a distant horizon or Sugarloaf Mountain, as the accomplishments of the visionary founder of St. F.X. would entitle him to do. He looks instead, across West Street, and down at the cairns that huddle between the street and the river there.

The Old Bishop looks sad. Maybe this is because he must stand there and watch drivers ignore the one way sign on the street up to the university and he knows there's going to be a wreck some day. Or maybe he wants them to put the letters back on his pedestal so people will know what he did when he was among the living. Or maybe he's like me, not sad but confused, because he can't figure out what to make of the cairns. What is a cairn? Who put them up? And why? And are more going to appear?

The Old Bishop has been there a good half century longer than the cairns, after all, though the cairns *look as if* they've been here a long time, too. Actually, the first one was put there during Highland Games Week in 1979, by the Chisholms. I remember my non-Scottish puzzlement.

On the base of the first one, it says, CHISHOLM. Above that are two legendary horned animals and two men, naked except for a wreath the artist has delicately placed over their loins, each carrying a fighting- or walking-stick. THE ARMS OF THE CHISHOLMS. On another face, there is a diamond shaped slab with stones embedded in it. It looks too practical to be merely ornamental; too pretty to be a message.

Twenty feet away stands the MACDOUGALL cairn. It has round stones where the Chisholms favoured flat ones. It, too, is about twelve feet high. The face toward the street informs us that one of its stones was taken from Dunollie castle in Scotland. It, too, has an inscription, this one commemorating a family that has served God and country.

The third is the prettiest and most mysterious. It is made of one lovely piece of huge rock. TOUCH NOT THE CAT - BOT A GLOVA the bold letters proclaim. And beneath the letters is a picture of the fierce cat one is not to touch. Engraved into the stone is the clan name, CHATTAN. Why not touch the cat? But I don't know who to ask. The Chattans, who put this lovely cairn in Antigonish, do not grace the phone book.

Those of us living here before there were cairns are like the monkeys in 2001 A.D., which began with monkeys frolicking in a rocky place, throwing a rock, grunting and putting grunts together, inventing communication, inventing the club, and doing monkey things. Then, one day there is amongst them, a monolith, a huge steel-looking object, unexplained, in their midst. The monkeys touch it, pray to it, quake in fear.

I didn't see any cairns go up. They just appeared, right where the Old Bishop is staring. Like the Old Bishop, they are Scottish, dignified, and not going anywhere.

Last spring I mentioned the cairns to a roomful of university seniors. They'd been walking past the cairns, two or more times a day, for four years and they never noticed them.

Walking toward Main Street from the Old Bishop and the cairns, you cross the bridge over the Brierly Brook, see on your right the new gazebo with a bright light on top of its pointed roof, and notice, if you wish to notice, the Antigonish Cenotaph standing on the post office lawn.

The Cenotaph I understand. I am accustomed to the sentiments inscribed on that stone. There are cenotaphs, statues, and scrolls, sailors and soldiers monuments, too. I'm no more alien to that monument than most of my neighbours are.

The Cenotaph is a product of my grandparents' generation. I knew those men and their wives. I knew another country's version of those men and their wives. They were solid people who married for life, paid their taxes without anger, raised their kids, and went to Church.

Dr. Walsh's shiny history gives only the dates they thought mattered, 1914-1918, inscribed by people blessedly ignorant of the fact their own children would fight an even bigger war a few years later. "The War to End All Wars," the history books tell us they said. He includes a photo with Ms. (Mrs. or Miss they'd have said) K. M. MacDonald's words. Can anyone look at the confident patriotism of her words and not suspect that the faith has been broken?

IN MEMORIAM
AGAINST THE YEARS
WE RAISE THIS SHAFT
OF NATIVE STONE
ENDURING AS OUR
EVERLASTING HILLS
—IT STANDS—
A PLEDGE TO SHOW
WE HAVE NOT BROKEN FAITH
WITH THOSE WHO FOUGHT
AND
THOSE WHO DIED
THAT
FREEDOM MIGHT LIVE ON

The Cenotaph has outlasted the sentiments carved on it.

Those people's lives had more duties and fewer pleasures than ours. They trusted people we no longer trust (politicians, for instance), and didn't think much of people we think are just fine (Germans, racial minorities). They practised a loyalty that makes us uncomfortable. The men went to war, and they came home injured or whole, but knowing something important had been accomplished.

On the other side are the names of the soldiers: Gillises, the MacDonalds, the MacGillivrays, the MacIsaacs, the DeCostes, MacLeans, MacEacherns, and Deloreys. All those nice families I will never know very well.

And, sad to say, there is something false about it. That is why I turn off the set on Remembrance Day when the CBC interviews and pontificates and plays "The Last Post," when the *Casket* puts the pictures of the war dead in the paper, when the *Chronicle-Herald* writes its editorials. It is not that I disagree with the sentiments. It's that I find them quaint. Pledges and shafts and everlasting hills and talk of not breaking faith are just not part of the way people think anymore. And, aside from these Remembrance Day observances, they have no place on the CBC either.

This is how war and fighting and soldiers were looked at in the early part of the century: the seriousness, the trust in authority, the willingness to believe in a good war. And time has shown something else. This mood, this war, this way of looking at things was part of other people's youths, not mine. It doesn't have much to do with the world I live in. And the CBC and the *Casket* and the *Chronicle-Herald* know this, but go ahead with this stern posture anyway.

The cenotaph had a place of honour at the junction where St. Ninian meets West Street when I came to Antigonish. When you wanted to pull onto West Street from St. Ninian's, you stopped behind the Cenotaph, peeked around it, then edged out, peeked again, and gunned it onto West Street. If someone was coming, you hoped they'd seen you before you disappeared behind the Cenotaph.

There was a wonderful editorial in the *Casket* that must have appeared while town council was debating the matter. It argued that the Cenotaph should not be moved because it forced people to drive very carefully in that busy area of St. Ninian and West Street, thereby preventing accidents.

Now, it's on the post office lawn. Ms. K. M. MacDonald's "shaft of native stone, raised against the years", is becoming pocked. The town, including me, probably broke trust in the late 1970s when the Cenotaph was moved from a spot that forced all of us to think about it at least once a day. And we break more trust every time we walk by it and we don't see it sitting there quietly on the post office lawn.

The Cenotaph is not the only anachronism on the post office lawn. But the other one I understand better. The Cenotaph is less out-dated than the metal sculptures, two of them, one in front of the parking meters, and one on the lawn.

Like me, the metal sculptures are relics from more exciting times. They represent the last blast of the 1960's. They celebrate protest, anger, marching with signs.

The post office, customs, immigration, all that used to be in the town hall is now contained in the new (circa 1970) post office. The sculptures, like the building itself, positively reek good theory. They wanted a people place. They wanted art by Canadian artists. They wanted people power, and it was still the 1960's. These things represent people at meetings; people with placards. Metal stick figures, designed to rust. Let the rust be part of the charm at the people place.

But people marching in the streets looked American. The sculptures were made of old transmission parts, wheel bases, tie rods, engine parts. These things might have a rich association in New York or Toronto, but in Antigonish they looked like the back 40. People were incensed by these ugly metal statues that looked like things you'd find in an auto salvage. There was a fuss, the *Casket* printed letters of protest.

The sculptures were planted, and there they remain. The 1960s are over. Protesting humanity wasn't the future, but the sculptures remain, often with a coke can or soft drink cup punched over one of the protruding tie rods.

It is a time warp of sorts. Carrying signs; going out into the world; let's get the job done; posters, placards, briefcases, one protester carrying a chair, all marching humanity and disorder. How could they have known, in 1969 when they built the new post office, that protesting humanity would date even more quickly than shafts of everlasting native stone?

No base plate, no words explaining, no identifying marks. The post office proclaimed — as a with-it 1970 post office should — the people's right to protest for orderly change.

This morning, just before sunrise on an August morning in an empty town, I am walking and looking at statues because I woke up, wide awake, at 3:37 a.m., according to the digital clock on the dresser. Rather than wake my wife, I am walking. I walked past the Old Bishop, the cairns, the Cenotaph, and headed for the town square, and the statue of the True Scots.

4

The True Scots glisten reddish in the light of the traffic signal that is suspended on a wire in the middle of the town square. Not a sound to be heard except the buzzing lights on a pole and the switch changing the colours of the stop light, and the odd car with lovers in it pulling up to the light, then screeching away, late. The moon is high and almost full; a single star shines above it. Clouds in the east loom dark and dramatic.

It is, incidentally, a politically correct work of the mid-1980s. A woman leads the horse, the man follows, pushing the plough. They are clearly Antigonish highland Scots. The husband (he is *clearly* a husband) wears a tam-o-shanter above his bib overalls. They are ploughing up the inclined pedestal. The horse has blinders, a big harness. It is much the biggest thing in the statue; then the plough, then the farmer; then the wife.

The Statue of the True Scots I love. I love it because I have been here longer than it has, because it was built with my tax money, because the mayor's generation of Antigonish Scots wanted this expression of their sense of the place.

Behind the sculpture is a small weedless garden—pansies in full flower, geraniums budding, and a softwood that must be spruce. Somebody cares about this statue. I am sitting on the bench made of 4x4 inch timbers placed in red brick. To my right is the main pedestal or support, also made of this red brick. It was erected in 1981, after the world had the benefit of the feminist movement, so it is non-sexist. Antigonish and I go back farther than Antigonish goes back with this statue. My taxes helped pay for it; and, the statue expresses me in spite of the words on its pedestal:

> From the lone shieling on the misty island,
> Mountains divide us and the waste of seas,
> But still the blood is true, the heart is highland,
> And in our dreams we see the Hebrides.[1]

I have played with the idea that my Scottish-Canadian neighbours long for Scotland the way I sometimes long for an Indiana town that I wouldn't return to if I could. I do not see signs of this dreaming in their faces, though I hear about it from wizened men in kilts during Highland Games Week, on Robert Burns's birthday, St. Andrew's Day, and at St. F.X.'s closing exercises. I am particularly not excited about the politics of kilts and

---

[1]As if to prove my point, my neighbours have misquoted the poem in a revealing way. Galt's words suggest something religious and wonderful about the Hebrides. He said, "*Behold*" the Hebrides.

cairns and a shouted love of Scotland. My Antigonish neighbours wear their kilts with a becoming quiet pride. To me, a kilt always says, "I am of this place and you are not." I realize it says other things, too, but it always says that.

It is not big as statues go, so it was placed on a four foot high brick platform. This brick platform, plus the wooden pedestal, brings the statue up to eye level.

The wooden pedestal was rotting from the rain and snow and fog that are a fact of life in Antigonish, and concerns were voiced about the durability of the statue itself. This problem was solved by putting a plastic cover around the statue and its pedestal. That way, the *Casket* reverently explained the town council's reasoning, the statue could sit outside all year in all kinds of weather so we Antigonishers could look at it in the winter when we paid our electric and water bills, and the tourists who strolled on Main Street could see it.

So there stood the Scot, the Wife, and the horse, all determinedly ascending the wooden pedestal, the rain beating down on the plastic cover, weathering the storm. But after the storm, when Antigonish was covered by blue sky and sunlight, the moisture that got inside the plastic caused condensation, and the statue steamed up. If you didn't know the Scot and his wife and horse were under the foggy cover, you'd never be able to guess. I personally felt that a statue that was foggy and unknowable even in the bright light of day was a good statue to have in front of the seat of Antigonish's town government. I saw the loving hand of the mayor — protecting the one horse town's one horse — with a protective case.

The town fathers and mothers had workers from the street department cut circular holes in the top at the front and back of the cover. Later, after the young men who sit on the bench beneath the statue late at night got into the habit of pushing their cigarette stubs through the air holes, the street department workers returned and covered the holes with mesh wire. If you stood back a little, the ventilating holes bore a not-unpleasing resemblance to those in the ticket window of the Capital Theatre across the street.

But, alas, as it always does in Antigonish, good sense prevailed. Today, the statue sits out there, uncovered, in all weather. I bumped into the mayor at Sobey's one morning. It couldn't have been 7:30, but there he was, this time in a grey windbreaker to match his grey hair and eyebrows. It was zipped up to his neck.

"Good morning, Your Worship," I said.

He'd seen me before. Give him a minute.

"Er...," he said.

"Phil," I said.

He acknowledged this. "Phil..."

"Milner," I added. "Phil Milner."

"Professor!" he said triumphantly. "From the college."

I told him I'd learned to like the protective cover, asked what had happened to it. He looked at me.

"That's been fixed." He caught my eye for the briefest second. He looked out the plate glass window, then down at his newspapers. The mayor would not fail to give history.

"That sculptor was quite a fellow," His Worship said.

"Oh, yeah," I said, waiting for more.

"He came here from Toronto," the mayor said.

I nodded.

"That fellow could put away the rum," His Worship said.

"I didn't know that," I said.

"Fellow must have started drinking on the airplane, and he was still drinking when we took him back to the airport."

I imagined pleasant afternoons in the council chambers.

"My taxes pay for that?" I asked.

His worship didn't reply, and I didn't push it, but I think he enjoyed the line. He flashed his self-absorbed smile. "Rum," after all, according to Bierce, is "a fiery liquor that produces madness in total abstainers."

Fall

The Professor Lectures His Daughter

Winning these weekly games of racketball gives me no particular pleasure, Daughter, and seeing you tie yourself in knots trying to beat me makes me wonder what either of us is trying to prove. Victory over your father will come, Daughter, and when it does, it will not be as sweet as you think it will be.

I want to tell you a story. It happened long ago in another country. The hero is 30 years old, and he has three children under the age of five, and a wife at home taking care of them. There may never have been a more earnest father than the hero of my story.

My hero is a writer. He writes articles for the Chicago papers, rates vehicles for *Camper Coachman*, investigates trailer deals for *RV Retailer*, does annual reports for any school board with a thousand dollars to pay him. Editors don't always want his articles, and when they do want them, they don't pay what they are worth. So the writer drives a 1964 Chevrolet that roars when he starts it, smokes when he climbs a hill, and keeps on running after he cuts the engine. He fills its tires with air every day. The writer is so poor that he must nod humbly when gas station attendants tell him he owes it to his family to buy new tires.

Four evenings a week from 11 at night until 7 the next morning, the writer puts on a blue uniform and a hat with a badge above the bill, and becomes a security guard. Sometimes he puts drunken students to bed. Sometimes he tells crowds of people to stand behind the rope. Sometimes people tell him to fuck off.

Most people think he is a security guard, but he tells himself and everyone else that he is a writer. And, since the world doesn't let him get away with many pretensions at this time of his life, we won't take it away from him just yet. We'll call him the Writer.

Let's give the Writer in our story some blue sky, a single billowing white cloud, a warm sunny day, and an perfect magazine assignment. He will boat down the Yellow River on a gorgeous summer day, photograph the sights, catch a carp, sleep in a tent, and write the experience up for the two million readers of a Sunday newspaper. The Writer borrows his father's aluminum boat, and he floats the boat 25 miles over two days down the lazy river.

When he lands, his father backs his pickup up to the river bank. The Writer pulls the tailgate down, and tries to lift the back end of the boat onto the pickup. He pulls and he puffs, but the boat falls, each time, onto the muddy bank. He can not lift that aluminum boat onto the pickup to save his soul.

"God damn it, stand to hell back," the Writer's father shouts, using a special voice full of contempt that only his wife and children ever hear. The father steps into the water in his shined street shoes, grabs the handles on the back of the boat, and flings it onto the pickup.

"See if you can rún the God damned rope through the bow, and throw it over to me," the father says. "See if you can do something right."

On the drive home, the Writer sulks. He keeps his thoughts to himself, but I will tell you what those thoughts were. The Writer cursed his father, and he wished him a thousand misfortunes. Not knowing the writer had put a curse upon him, the father talked about the weather, about the Cubs's chances of winning the pennant, about a fellow he knew in Wabash.

The story jumps forward fifteen years, and moves to another country. You know some of the rest, Daughter. That nice old man you always tell me I should be nicer to, the one whose diabetic eyes light with love behind his thick new glasses when you walk into the room, the one who tells you stories about me that make me sound like Einstein and Gretzky rolled into one? Well, that old guy is the father in the pickup. That old man who tells you all those stories about how great his son is never never said "I love you" to his son. Not once.

And the seething thirty year old writer who cursed his father with an adolescent's powerless passion? Well, some money and human kindness, fifteen years of good luck and a job that gives him a lot of unearned respect have changed him, Daughter. He'd like to think they've changed him beyond recognition.

You know that man, too, and we've almost finished with him. Frankly, his hopefulness, his belief that his hard work would make a difference, and his trust in the power of love all embarrass me.

Before we put him away forever, there are some morals to this story, Daughter. I promise to be quick. I know you'd rather be somewhere else, so stop twisting the handle of your duffel bag around your hand or you'll cut off your circulation.

The first moral is that curses work. All the curses that the impotent writer uttered against his father came true. The writer's father pees with pain, can't turn his head without wincing, and its all he can do to push himself out of his chair. Today, he couldn't lift that boat if his life depended on it.

The second moral is that beating your father is the work of the first third of your life. But once you beat him, and you will, Daughter, you won't lose to him again.

But here is the strangest moral. The Writer would lift his curse if he could. He would like nothing better than to see his father wade up a river with a fly rod in his hand again; or drink six bottles of beer on a Sunday afternoon again.

In fact, the writer would like to throw his arms around his father, tell his father that he forgives him, and ask his father to forgive him a few things too. But that is not how the writer and his father work.

There's another moral here, daughter; I'll say it and you can be on your way. The Writer loves you like he loves the air he breathes. And even though words are his bread and butter, he can't seem to say that to you any better than his father could say it to him.

The time is coming when you'll win that racketball game and some other games, too. The writer won't mind. He knows who he is, after all, and winning racketball games is not where its at for him.

But he's scared. He is afraid he will lose you like his own father lost him.

3 Lighting Fires

> *"Every man looks at his woodpile with a kind of affection. I loved to have mine before my window, and the more chips the better to remind me of my pleasing work. I had an old axe which nobody claimed, with which by spells in winter days, on the sunny side of the house, I played about the stumps which I had got out of my bean-field. As my driver prophesied when I was ploughing, they warmed me twice, once when I was splitting them, and again when they were on the fire, so that no fuel could give out more heat."*
>
> — Henry David Thoreau, *Walden*

The paper match flares, and I touch it to the newspaper under the spruce kindling. A minute later I add a bigger piece of spruce, finally a stove length of split maple. A hint of smoke and spruce rises. September is a month of small pleasures. By April, when the students leave and the snow pretty well has stopped, there is no joy in wood smoke or making fires.

The house had been bought and sold three times in the four years before we bought it. When the wind howled on winter nights, I watched snow blow through our unheated bedroom. We crammed insulation into the holes in the walls, put styrofoam over the clapboards, and vinyl siding over that. We borrowed money and replaced rotted windows. We installed one woodstove, then two more. For two years, my family peed and showered at the gym on cold mornings because water pipes were frozen, while Richard the carpenter made heroic interventions at reasonable prices.

If winter is hard, spring almost justifies the life we live. On the hill across the road I stripped the sod, sprinkled manure from Ikemoto's horses, spaded, roto-tilled, and harvested strawberries, gooseberries, raspberries, and currants. I watched my neighbour, Netta-san, gather eggs from the barn that marks the edge of her property. I helped her, one November Saturday, kill the rats that threatened her chickens.

I heard again and again the history of the property line that divides their properties from mine. I nodded as my neighbours told their story of property lines, betrayal, a lost or altered will to the property I had bought, conniving lawyers, pages razor bladed from the town records. The thirty-year feud was over land, and then over everything else, too.

But I was exempt. My neighbours tolerated my car-chasing dog, the woodpile I lacked the skill to organize, the April grass fire I started that killed the fir windbreak between Ikemotos and the Connors. I tolerated Netta-san's collapsing barn, and the anti-social actions of her son, whom I suspect poisoned our cat. Ike-san and his son fixed my water pump when it stopped pumping. The neighbour above ploughed my garden, gave me raspberry canes, shoveled my drive with his tractor and blade. I gave them great quantities of my unmarketable honey. I said nothing to the neighbour who put Round Up on the soil above my well and his. The quality of kindness dare not be strained among neighbours in the country.

Technically, our house is on the road's right-of-way, but the house was there before the road was. There is a squared off poor man's bay window on the north side, four towering old cedars in front of our veranda.

The back of the house faces the river, the hill rolling away, apple trees, a wheat field, with an island of alders and chokecherry, and one huge elm. In the autumn deer nibble at the apples. Grosbeaks, flickers, thrushes, cedar wax wings eat the berries and rose hips. Skunks appear at night in spring; raccoons and squirrels set up shop near the bird feeder. We bought books, looked them up, and learned to identify ospreys, eagles, three kinds of grosbeak, goldfinches, orioles, and pine siskins. We reclaimed our first serious garden from the cooch grass and Queen Anne's lace. Non-descript willows grow in the swamp that forms below the house during the spring thaw. In the shed, I found a metal stencil, WILLOWBANK FARMS, with white paint on the edges. The orchard on the hill above the house features a dozen out of control apple trees. The youngest trees just happened. They grew out of the rotting trunks of their predecessors, or birds shat them. They have strange tasting apples. One produces yellow apples in August.

The property survey I commissioned in a vain attempt to remain above the neighborhood border feud calls the road Cunningham Road, after the first owners of our house. Norm Cunningham raised chickens, sold eggs, and ran an implement store. When his will was probated, Netta-san insisted someone had taken a razor blade to the page in the plat book that gave her the house. The other neighbor was given ten square feet of Cunningham property to dig his well on.

During our first winter, 1985, nobody climbed out of bed in our house until the absolute last minute. Then, my wife and kids hurried to the St. F.X. gym for showers. Evenings we huddled around the single wood stove, which warmed the family room, and nothing else. In December of our first year we bought a propane tank with an attached heater. We feared an explosion. The kitchen smelled like a swimming pool. Because of the dark fir panelling, it was impossible to make the house bright. Because the house is really two houses, joined by hallways, we added two more wood stoves to keep it warm between November and April. The house is so big and ramshackle that oil or electric heat would be impractical.

My coffee pot is on the wood stove beside the word processor. At seven, an alarm buzzes upstairs. Footsteps. A toilet flushes, the water pump begins its throaty pumping. Voices waft down, distant and strident. Early September is a good time of year.

"Are you going to stay in there all day? It's my turn in the bathroom."

"Where's the blow dryer? Beth never puts anything back."

"Why is it so cold?"

"It frosted last night. Look at the windshield!"

"Everything's silver outside!"

"You were the last one up last night. Why didn't you put wood on?"

"Who used all the hot water?"

"You were in there a half hour? Can't you take a quick shower when you know other people need to use it?"

"You're wearing my new sweater."

"You said I could."

"Once. I said you could wear it once, not every day."

"I've only worn it twice! Yesterday and today."

"That's once too many."

"You wear my penny loafers. I can't find them. You put them in your closet. Where are they?"

"I loaned them to Marlene."

A door swishes, the smell of lavender and hair.

At ten before eight Paul appears in the doorway, hair wet, new jeans and plaid shirt, kisses me on the cheek, opens the door, and looks for the bus, exactly as he did last spring. I hear the bus rumble on the other fork. He shouts and dashes for Ikemoto's. Jiggs sneaks out the door, and chases the bus up the hill and around the bend, his bark menacing and triumphant. Hasty kisses, and the females depart.

This year the first fire converges with the pre-registration meeting of the English Department. Tanned and robust, my gut and drinking habit are gone for now. I look forward to the department meeting. My colleagues will be rested and full of hopeful schemes today. Today they will be glad to see me. No haggard and gray faces; no paranoid rants. My colleagues are witty and I like some of them.

2

The registration line snakes slowly toward the gym in the afternoon sunshine, but the students don't seem to mind. They are dancing to ghetto blasters, comparing notes about courses, throwing footballs, catching up with each other on the summer. When they get inside, my colleagues and I hand them computerized course stickers that look like they belong on cans in a supermarket.

On the first day of classes, I make my little professorial jokes. Students laugh. My syllabus promises a feast for the intellect: Emily Dickinson, *The Scarlet Letter*, Walt Whitman, Thoreau's *Walden*, Whittier's *Snowbound* and *Uncle Tom's Cabin*. I explain about papers and tests and tell how to score a 90. Are there any questions? I ask. There are, and they are intelligent. It promises to be a great year.

In November, male students stop shaving. Women forsake makeup. Faces become pallid. Even the pre-meds in the front rows wander to my 8:15 class through the morning darkness with their shoes untied. December tests confirm what students feared. It is a war of attrition, and they have been assigned to a chickenshit outfit.

In January my suffering troops are passing around viruses they brought back from Christmas vacation. I wonder how they hear me above the sound of their coughing.

"I don't know whether I should lecture you or conduct you," my colleague across the hall told his Shakespeare class.

In February, the room smells of disinfectant, fumes from the oil furnace, disappointment and paranoia. Student papers show signs of haste, critical re-hash, sometimes outright plagiarism.

By March my ragged platoon is pasted against the back wall. I ask a question. The two pair of eyes that were on my face drop to the floor. I answer the question myself. It was a stupid question anyway.

During office hours, the captain hears confessions. A paper on Bartleby the Scrivener is late because the student's father left her mother, who is having a nervous break-down. Another student's girlfriend broke up with him the night before the paper was due and he has been walking around in a fog ever since. But he can have the paper in by Friday. Someone's grandmother died; a paper was lost; a notebook was stolen.

One student told me that she was carrying her paper on Walt Whitman from the Annex when the wind came up and blew it from her hand. She chased it across the parking lot and saw it sailing over the football field toward the Trans-Canada Highway. I gave her the extension she requested. I lost a hat to that wind once. Others report confrontations with the dean, harassment by the business office, conflicts with other professors.

King Solomon himself could not determine which of these stories are true. Try to judge them and your office will be like tryout night for an amateur play. Word goes out that the professor wants to be convinced. If your boyfriend dropped you and you want your deadline extended, the professor wants tears. If you have a severe cold and cannot take the test, he wants to hear a cough from deep in the lungs. If your grandfather died and you're on your way to the funeral, he wants to see stoic acceptance in your face and you in your Sunday best.

A colleague, riding the elevator, overheard one student tell another how to get his professor, a priest, to extend a deadline for a theology paper:

"Tell him you think you're losing your faith."

But cynicism is corroding, and unworthy of one's high calling to the life of the mind. Another student read Thoreau's Walden and realized that a university town in the rural Maritimes is exactly the right place to replicate Thoreau's experiment. He found an abandoned shack in a field overlooking George's Bay on the Harbour Road. Now he hitch-hikes to classes, burns wood in a small stove and feels the salt and wind through his un-puttied windows as he reads his assignments. I suspect he knows more about the real cost of enlightenment than most of his professors.

My students write papers totalling 50 pages or more. If they carry five arts classes, they will write 200 pages of papers in an academic year. I write words like "pretentious" and "awkward" in the margins; I circle misspellings. I would be insulted if my friends were as candid when they detected my intellectual pretensions. I could not write well under the pressures I put on my students.

Studying for my test on Whitman's Song of Myself while researching a philosophy paper on Plato's concept of the beautiful and memorizing the periodic table for Chemistry 100 is only part of what they must do for tomorrow.

They also help the chaplain organize retreats, drink beer, attend dances, go to games and concerts, line up dates for Friday night. They operate a student government that has as much energy, betrayal and confusion as the one in Ottawa. They put out a student newspaper that is surprisingly professional, though university administrators tend to be as thin-skinned and vindictive as Haitian dictators. Students wedge the overcrowded academic year inside their overcrowded extra-curricular year.

An academic year has eight months. A week has five days. An hour has 50 minutes. All learning — from The Plays of Shakespeare to a course on playing saxophone in a jazz band — is crammed into 50-minute or 75-minute slots (with time for questions at the end).

Each tick of the clock is measured, dissected, and pretended to be something larger than it is. Could anyone except a baffle of university administrators have created such a calendar? We faculty and administrators deserve the misshapen fruit — Coles Notes and the BS Unlimited Term Paper Co. are representative examples — that the system we operate has spawned.

In early May, the last students load their ghetto blasters, books, posters and clothing into cars and head home to Glace Bay, West Bay, New Glasgow, Toronto, Calgary or North Adams, Mass.

After they leave, I put in my garden. I turn the cold earth with my shovel, then roto-till it, sprinkle on some of my neighbor's horse manure, decide what goes where, and plant the seeds. Here in northern Nova Scotia, winter lets go grudgingly; I cannot put my tomatoes out until the middle of June. If I put them out before that, the frost kills them. The growing season has its own cycle. Days have 24 hours, weeks seven days. You can't rush things in a garden.

It is pleasant work, and it leaves me time to ask my question. Why did my own and my students' clear-eyed best dry up sometime in November?

But for now, it is still September. As always, I begin in hope. I know there are blackberries in Netta-san's secret patch (she showed me where it was when we were still speaking). I sneak over under cover of twilight and get some. Red berries on bushes, crows and gulls, mud holes, ruts, an osprey wheeling overhead. The smell of apples is in the cooling air. Though it is almost the middle of September, it felt like high summer all day. At seven in the evening it is still warm. I'd forgotten the fading red in the west and gold here where I'm picking. It makes an Antigonish autumn the loveliest anywhere.

3

When I came here, from a land where a certain amount of posturing is viewed as a citizen's birthright, I was puzzled by the results of the first examinations. Students for whom I could call up no faces whatsoever had written the best examination papers. They had obviously mastered the material, but they had not been moved to ask questions, to challenge my interpretations, to show me poems or short stories that they had written, or to do the other things that outstanding American students did when they took English classes.

The next day I singled out the faceless authors of those excellent tests. They seemed as embarrassed as they were pleased by the public attention that their accomplishments brought.

When I asked where they were from, they flashed smiles that were unique to this place. The smiles said this: "You probably won't care, but it is nice of you to act interested." Then they'd say, "I'm a Caper," or "I'm from East Bay" or "From Mabou," or St. Peters or Cheticamp or Glace Bay, and they would nod to the friends from the same place who stood in a half circle behind them, wearing identical hockey jackets and similar friendly and embarrassed expressions.

Only after I had lived here a few years did I realize that the smile said something else, too. "Humble as I am, I might know a few things that a person like yourself hasn't thought of."

But by the time I figured that out, I was using the smile myself, and reacting with bemused tolerance to the airs of Ontarians and Englishmen and other Americans.

I have observed those deferential students in their candid moments — as guests in my home, in their senior seminars, in their cups at the Triangle Tavern or the Golden X — and I can tell you that they understand their professors very well indeed. In Antigonish, nobody will tell you that you are being pompous, complacent, obnoxious, or that you have a loud mouth.

"If you want to make a fool of yourself," a friend told me after a mutual friend had made a complacent and self-serving speech at a Church meeting, "people in Antigonish will let you."

My years in the Maritimes have not made me a better person, but they have made me a less visibly aggressive person. I am a person who is more careful not to be caught posturing than my training and instincts prepared me to be. This is because I know my pretensions, my moral failings, my affectations, and all the boasts that I do not deliver on will be noted and chuckled over by a lot of other people. None of them will feel that they ought to let me in on the humour of my behavior.

This familiarity cuts another way. When you live day in and day out with the same people, you learn that their virtues and shortcomings are simply different spots on the same tapestry. The man who hogged the middle of the racquetball court and then smashed me in the small of the back with the ball on Wednesday brings my injured ten-year old home from a softball game on Saturday, after he has spent two hours of his own time waiting in the out-patient room because he couldn't get hold of me. The man who cut me off in the Jim's One Stop parking lot last Thursday is standing beside me at the eleven o'clock mass on Sunday. If I shook my fist at him in the parking lot, we will both dread the kiss of peace. I learn that the colleague who said such savage things about me at a dinner party, and whom I have been giving the cold shoulder to ever since I heard, has a daughter with leukemia; my frosty pride is revealed to me as the unworthy thing that it is. Everyone's virtues and vices are more or less public here. The lesson of small-town life is that we are all in this together.

4

Raymie MacPherson's ten-wheeler sat in my yard, across the road from my house, piled high with seven cords of wood and a tree loader. Ike-san stood on the ground, waving.

"Lots of wood ok," Ike-san said. "I tell Clyde put where put last year, ok?"

Last year Raymie delivered 14 cords of wood. He told me I'd like it because there wasn't much to split. There wasn't. It burned like match sticks. I spent my winter evenings replenishing my wood stoves. The coffee lounge is full of stories by professors who feel they have been duped. That was my contribution to the literature for last year.

Ike-san told me to complain, so I reminded Raymie of last year's wood when I placed my order. With Ike-san's friendly but watchful assistance, Clyde lovingly set my 14 cords of thick eight foot lengths into two neat piles near the back door, and this third pile across the road.

"How about a little nip, Ike-san?" I asked after Clyde left.

"Maybe ok," Ike-san said. "Splash-splash."

I half-filled two coffee cups with Jack Daniels.

"Corn whiskey," Ike-san said. "Not drink often. Twice before. With you. American."

"Bourbon," I said.

We sipped.

"Good wood ok."

"It is, isn't it? I'm glad you were here, Ike-san. You know the difference."

"We good neighbours, Milner-san. You know that we'd do anything for you, yeah."

I never knew what to say when Ike-san said that. I looked for irony in his friendly brown eyes. I suspect Ike-san judges intelligence and character by one's ability with a chainsaw. Ike-san knew everything there was to know about trees and saws, though fifty years in Antigonish had not taught him or his wife Netta-san the subtleties of the English language. More than once he responded to the wail of my saw against hardwood, and came over to talk about weather and life, and then sharpened my chainsaw before he left. For weeks afterwards, cutting wood was like cutting butter. Ike-san once spent three days helping my children and me split and stack 14 cords of hardwood. Giving him money seemed insulting, so I gave him great quanties of the duty-free bourbon I and my family would pick up whenever we crossed the border.

"Number one saw. Husquvarna best," Ike-san said.

"Sharp as I can make it," I said. Ike-san didn't smile.

I rolled my splitting block, almost a yard across, to Ike-san to sit on.

Ike-san has skin the colour of creamed coffee, a long red drinker's nose, a plaid mackinaw, no hat winter or summer under his full head of graying black hair. There's never been a winter he didn't get a deer, though the first one is the only one he talks about. He is consistently more right about the weather that the ATV weather man.

"I make cutting block for Mrs. Jeffirs when she live here?" Ike-san said. Whatever he said seemed to be stated as a question. "Big elm, wakaru?"

Ike-san is at least twenty-five years older than I am. He calls juncos snowbirds, and bald eagles -- which are plentiful around here because Ike-san feeds them raccoon and muskrat carcasses after skinning, deer or pig carcasses after butchering -- he calls king fishers.

We pretend that neither of us knows my precarious woodpile will topple within a week, as though we both know that salmon lie in that shady spot underneath Tommy MacInnis's wire and not on the bend where I was fishing, as though we both knew all along that the time and place to catch ocean trout is on a rapids when the wild strawberries are blooming, as though it were an eccentric professor's experiment that led me to put tomatoes north of the corn row where the sun can't reach them.

Putting aside what I hear, which I only half believe; and the neighbourhood women's general distrust of Ike-san; which he earned long before my time, he's the best of neighbours. Netta-san, tells me not to give him booze.

"So! Too much Captain Morgan," she says, pointing at *my* stomach. "Make you fat, make Ike sick, wakaru?"

In October pickups pull up to the shed next to Ike-san and Netta-san's chicken coop, and orange-coated men unload their deer. Sometimes they pull a live pig off a truck by its tail. Then a gunshot. Later, the men, glassy eyed and smelling of rum, dignified but not unfriendly, silently carry carcasses to the riverbank, while Ike-san washes his hands in the horsetank.

Last winter Ike-san's eldest daughter died of a brain haemorrhage.

"Only the good die young." I heard that several times. Ike-san stayed sober that week as we wandered in and out of his house bearing our hot casseroles, biting back tears, making bright conversation. The night she died, someone shot two of Mr. denHovel's cows, slit the tires on the passenger side of my pickup, and two more tires at the student apartment on the hill. People blamed Ike-san, of course, their only evidence being his odd ways.

"I have more elm blocks over there. Some big ones ok," Ike-san says. "You take your pick. You good neighbour, Mr. Milner."

Suddenly Netta-san appeared. Ike-san set his coffee cup under the steps, and put his foot in front of it.

"How'd you like to have a Chinaman for a neighbour?" Netta-san asked me.

"I'd probably like it just fine," I said.

"So! You think Chinese and Japanese same-same, Milner-san," Netta-san said. "Japanese good neighbours for sure," she said.

In a town where Cape Bretoners are considered outsiders, our street is absolutely alien. My family is American. The Davis's are English and American. Ikemotos are the only Japanese family in town, and I know they have suffered for their accent.

"I hear Mike Lee's all right," I said.

"Chinese not Japanese, wakaru?"

She ambled back toward her house. Ike-san fished his coffee cup out from under the steps, took a sip, and motioned toward the collapsed barn.

"Mike Lee not to buy land on flood plain," Ike-san said when his sister was out of earshot. "That bullshit about Mike Lee. I'm married to crazy woman. No wonder I drink, you know?" Ike-san said.

"I help Babe Cunningham buy a new car when she lived here," Ike-san said. "She pick it out. I teach her drive it. She said someday I could have it. So when she die...," Ike-san nodded toward the house above us. "...He take. Ike-san pointed toward his collapsed barn. "He go right in there and take. That not right, is it?"

"When was that, Ike-san?"

"That be...That be October..." Ike-san said, and his watery almond eyes narrowed. "October of '49."

Almost a half century ago, and the principles are still living here, in the neighborhood, remembering, still summoning the angry fires from a half-century ago.

"Well, must go now; you know," he said.

"Good, then!" I said.

Ike-san trudged away. I looked up to see my neighbour from above, negotiating the path. He must have been waiting for Ike-san to leave.

"Nice wood," he said. "Big. You split that, and you'll have some burning this winter." He looked at my saw. "Husquvarna," he said. "I have Jonsered, looks a lot like yours. He ran his fingers over the chain. "Do you have a brace?"

"What's that?" I asked.

"It fits on the chain, and then you sharpen every tooth exactly the same. Maybe, you'd like to borrow my brace."

"I have a guide," I said.

"Braces are better," he said. "They take the guess-work out of it."

The times Ike-san had sharpened my saw, the first thing he did was remove the guide I had attached to my file, and dropped it on the ground contemptuously. Ike-san kept his heavy old saws throwing big wide wood chips. He didn't need it, and he didn't approve of it. My neighbour looked at the wood pile, stepped back, cocked his head and turned his eyes to the bottle on the deck.

"How about a nip?" I said.

"Bourbon," he said, and he made a face. "Nothing personal, but that stuff takes like cough medicine to me."

"I have a bottle of the Captain inside," I said.

He smiled.

"Cape Breton Holy Water," he said. "Better not." He looked at me, and back at the wood pile. "Kind of dangerous cutting," he said. 'I notice you don't wear the pants."

"No, I never bought a pair."

"I wear safety pants all the time. They're double thickness, and if the saw gets away ... a saw can't get through them. One year I misplaced them and bought another pair. If you'd like, I'll sell them at a real good price."

"Well, maybe I'll stop up and look at your brace, too," I said.

"I saw Ike-san walking up the lane," he said.

"He helped unload," I said.

"You give him a drink?"

5

Students do as they are told. We assign their tasks, judge the quality of what they produce at our behest. It is an old and honorable system. To work, it needs only for us to be wise in our use of our incredible power, sincere in our committment to teaching, and honest in our methods.

When I was a student, there were old professors who cared mostly about the biographies of writers. The great poets saw more and felt more deeply than the rest of us do, these professors told us. They were wiser than we are. We should read their poems and study their lives in order to learn the lessons about life that the great poets can teach us.

I, and other smart English majors, sneered at them behind their backs, and followed the lead of our young professors, who also sneered at their older colleagues. The young professors called themselves "new critics," and they taught us smart English majors that literature made a world of its own (microcosm). We smart English majors studied that world with the dispassion of geologists analyzing rocks. We found form, paradox, structure, internal principles, metaphors, paradigms. I became a professor myself. When I wasn't doing something else, I was doing that.

By now, I am almost as old as the professors I sneered at. Father MacSween, the oldest practicing professor I ever saw, put his own twist on biographical material. I borrowed some of his ideas, learned a few new ones, came to almost understand a few of my own obsessions.

Why shouldn't the smart young professors sneer at me? When they do theory, or semiotics, structuralism, deconstruction, reader-based criticism, worry about re-defining the canon, I don't sneer back. Literature goes on. Criticism is harmless. In ten years it is all forgotten, all except that written by the poets and novelists themselves.

Good teaching is hard to measure and too easy to fake. It involves integrity, knowledge, and sincerity. A lot of people invested a lot of time and energy providing students and professors with student evaluations of their courses. After ten years of being "evaluated," of looking through mounds of computer printouts and comments on my teaching, I have decided that I have something to say. Student evaluations of professors are almost worthless.

This is unfortunate for students, for professors, and for learning.

Course evaluations cease being a low energy joke only after the forms are completed. Then, the entire bureaucratic structure of the university springs to life. The forms are fed to the Hewlett-Packard, tabulated, charted, averaged, analyzed, and published in the *Weekly*. Unfortunately, garbage quantified is still garbage.

I watched students fill out the course evaluation forms for some of my less shameless colleagues. Some students blacked in the #1 slot all the way through the computerized answer sheet. *** Highly Recommended, as the published booklet has it. A few scowled, and awarded a row of 6's. Not Recommended. Others, knowing that something more was asked for, punched something between one and six for the first third of the evaluation, then quickly slashed three dozen terminal 3's. ** Moderately Recommended. Then, the non-computerized comment section: what did you like best about this course? "Course evaluation day because I didn't have to listen to Milner gassing."

I would have been more pleased with my two triple stars if students had not bestowed them on the curators of bird courses (bribery pays), crowd pleasers (cheap theatre pays), snake-oil salespeople (so does pandering to student prejudices), the local operators who say that St. F.X. is the only university in the world that cares about its students (demagoguery pays), and those affable hangers-on who have, in a phrase I learned from a friend who teaches at UNB, "retired in place" (True Maritimers, our students are suckers for nice folks).

In my creative writing class, students complained about workload and methodology to whoever would listen. The Dean dutifully tried to thwart my best effort. Those triple stars were my only public vindication. Student comments showed that they knew where I went wrong. Criticism is not a disloyal activity.

My American lit class, "** Moderately Recommended", was a failure. After a summer of reading writers I hadn't thought about since grad school, I thought I had important things to say about Michael Wigglesworth, Joel Barlow, Sarah Kemble Knight, and 51 others. I had decided in a flush of August idealism that students should see the wildflowers that Emerson talked about and feel the cold that Jack London wrote about. Toronto and Ottawa have better libraries, but St. F.X. and Antigonish, like nineteenth-century Harvard and Concord, have a human-sized university surrounded by an outdoor landscape that the march of North American commerce has not got around to taming.

I ignored funny looks from students, looked past the ironic smiles of the Dryasdusts, and English 244 went to the woods. I wanted students to encounter the radiance Thoreau found in his rural environment. They wanted to know what would be on the test. I wanted students to write what they saw in nature after reading writers who saw multitudes there. They thought I wanted them to write that birds were beautiful, that the smell of chicory gave them goosebumps, that the sight of the West River helped them unwind after a hard day of hitting the ole books.

By November, my charge of righteous energy was flagging. By January, students were sitting on their hands in ennui. My lectures reeked of self-pity, fatigue, and suppressed anger.

Course evaluation week was their revenge.   I permitted the *Weekly* to publish just how bad it was, even though I was given four opportunities to prevent publication.   I was asked to give my consent for my students to fill out the evaluation form in early April. A month later I was asked if it would be all right for the students union to run them through the computer. A month after that granted permission for the *Weekly* to publish its computerized tabulation. Then, someone wrote a summary that put the best face that could be put on the disaster of English 244, and I was asked to ok that.

While respect for one's elders is generally a good thing, it is not the first commandment.

Here is my suggestion. Tell the graduating seniors, during senior week, that there is free beer and a live band at the Inn, but that some of them might wish instead to answer these three questions about teaching effectiveness in a test booklet:

1) What courses and professors and texts helped you learn?
2) Where did the university waste your time and energy?
3) Do you have any suggestions to improve the system?

Give the volunteers three hours and lots of test booklets. Then find two graduating honours seniors with independent minds, a feel for language, and demonstrated integrity. Give them a fraction of the money now spent on forms, paper, computer time, miniature golf pencils, secretarial support, and administrative harrumphing to edit the results. Finally, get the writer/editors out of town before the evaluations are published. There will be no thanks for doing this job right.

This is money that is being wasted. Students could buy beer or books with it, increase the photo-copying budget with it, or lure even more famous rock bands from even farther away with it. They might even try to conduct a meaningful evaluation of university teaching with some of it.

6

It is late Friday afternoon, registration complete, classes not yet begun. I have 97 students, the fewest I've ever had, among them 14 seminar students, who are among the best I've ever had. The ones who have taken classes from me before are all students I am glad to be working with again. I feel old and benign. Jiggs sits at my feet, gnawing at his genitals.

I am heading to Chevy's to drink beer with my new colleagues. I was invited for an outing with the young faculty. Antigonish comes as close to solving the loneliness problem as a town can come. All this can make you complacent. I think I have seen people who move from the coffee lounge to the rink to the dinner party to the Oland Centre to the Triangle Tavern to the Snow Queen to the Library Lounge, and seem oblivious to the fact that they were born alone and will die alone.

I arrive at Chevy's and find my colleagues. Eight of them are gathered around a table, drinking beer and eating soggy corn chips smothered in cheese and peppers, which they bought and paid for long before I got there. I sit at the head of the table, the only seat available. I am 15 years older than anybody else at the table. I shake hands. Mostly, these are faces I have been seeing but not speaking to on elevators and at the mail room.   Faces and names that I almost know, but cannot put together.

I shake hands and fall into my comfortable Antigonish posture of pretending I have never seen them before in my life.   I flash my affable I'm-no-threat Antigonish smile.   I down three quick beers and try to contribute to the nice mood.

I know the waitress, a friend of one of my kids. This impresses the young faculty seated down the table from me.   In fact I know almost everyone in the place except the professorati I am sitting with.

"Of course, for Phil Milner, Antigonish *is* the world" wafts up the table to me.   It is a bearded philosopher speaking more loudly than he'd meant to.   To him I look like a local.

Silence.

Then, a political scientist with his hair in a pony tail comes to my defense.

"Phil Milner's not from here."

"Oh," says the stricken philosopher.   "Thanks *a lot*," he whispers to my defender.   "I suppose this'll cost me tenure."

I have been in Antigonish for almost twenty years. To an outsider, I look and sound and act like a native. To a local, I look and sound and act like an American. Words start coming out of my mouth.

"Of course, you have to get away from here sometimes.   I need to get to Halifax at least once a month," I say loudly and irrelevantly to Jane, my office mate.

Do I believe what I am saying? Do I go to Halifax once a month for the plays, restaurants, art galleries, better libraries, movies and high culture? And what an idle defense if I do? To someone from Toronto or France (the handsome couple at the middle of the table teach French). Halifax once a month as proof of my urbanity!

My office is in Martha Place, where above my head I hear the tap tap tap of the nuns in their leather heels. Outside my office door nursing instructors communicate in friendly words and mostly female laughter, as we five people move back and forth from offices to the windowless unisex washroom, where the stool sits on a platform ten inches above the floor under an overhead light.

The hubbub from Nicholson Hall rings sweetly as a distant chain saw. Unlike Nicholson Hall, my two office windows open and let light and air in. The air here is not re-cycled. Light and air have a hard time of it over there. I look out one window and see three black smoke stacks that throw soot and provide heat. Out the other window, I see the library. My students wave as they pass my ground floor office.

Wilfred, my last office mate, was caught up and spit out (the jury is still out) by our unofficial hobby of back room politics.

I can be banished only with the greatest difficulty. A tenured professor doesn't have to seem to be a good teacher or bright-eyed colleague. The down-side of tenure is that after decades of calculating, and pulling punches as a non-tenured assistant professor, and a third of a lifetime before that of crafting insights to the irrelevant demands of irrelevant journals, teachers, professors, graduate advisors, and the occasional half-mad departmental chair, finding something authentic to teach is no simple task.

The English Department was like the Vietnam-era American army; fat and complacent and arrogant with too much power in too few people's hands. I would put on my blue blazer and tasteful grey tie, then make forays to the Nicholson Hall xerox machine, usually under cover of darkness. Wilf, on the other hand, commanded (not exactly the word) from Martha Place a ragtag platoon that operated from the very heart of the English Department. He would settle for nothing less than the university confessing its hypocrisy, ending its wedding to the very Ph.D. degree that has made my own professional life such a comfortable one. My objectives were humbler. I simply wanted to regain my teaching vocation, make my American literature course click, preserve my creative writing course from the Dryasdusts; while finding a way to write sincerely.

Wilf was Ho Chi Minh, going with inadequate troops against a superior army. The phone on his desk, in my outer office, would ring and ring. Sometimes, I'd pick it up. CBC calling; Toronto calling; a faculty association Pooh Bah calling. They wanted briefs, position papers, interviews.

I had published two little books in my ambitious phase that got me tenure and let me posture as a writer. I have as much to answer for as anyone. I know I will hear only praise for this book (as I heard only praise for those other books). The greasy postcard on the bulletin board with the bounced cheques at Gerard's Post Road ESSO, says, IF YOU LIKE OUR WORK, TELL YOUR FRIENDS. IF YOU DON'T LIKE IT, TELL US.

But it doesn't work that way. Polite to a fault, my ears will hear praise from my neighbours. Or nothing at all.

4 Himself

In lapidary inscriptions a man is not under oath.
— *Dr. Johnson* to *Boswell*

What was I doing at this feast of my enemies on this rainy autumn afternoon in this tiny Church? I was there because this is Antigonish County, where even a consummate injustice collector must work to keep anger and contempt alive when your enemies's kids are your kids's friends, when you see them at Church, in the mall, in the coffee lounge, and they are on the same committees you are on.

Of course Father MacSween would be the homilist. He sat at the altar, occasionally dabbing his forehead with a handkerchief, too sick to participate in the procession.

My wife and I sat on the bride's side, on the left with the MacSweenites. His former students, colleagues of mine, sat around me. Michael prayed dramatically in the third row, Judith all but invisible beside him. John and Jane Brine sat in dignity beneath the balcony. Mary's giggle rose above the pre-mass bustle, Richard beside her looking mildly worried and embarrassed; Bill smiling in bemusement as Cabrini's laughter trilled over the Church. I knew these people well from another time in my life.

There had been a time when Father MacSween gave me books, smoothed my way with the university power structure, put my name on the masthead of his *Antigonish Review*, took me for drives around the Landing, sprung me to huge meals at the priest's dining hall. After our falling out, he had me dropped from his *Review* and stopped speaking to me. "The MacSweenites," I called them, a monolithic block of locals who resisted the True Light (Professionalism! That's what it had been about), which I in my braveness, held aloft for all to follow.   Recently, Father MacSween had softened to the point of raising a hand in pained recognition when he drove his big Pontiac past me.

A squawk of bagpipes announced the wedding mass was to begin. The father-of-the-bride came forward beside his wife, who carried their daughter's baby. Except for my turmoil, it would be a wedding like all weddings.

"If I have not love, I am nothing," the celebrant intoned. "Love is patient and kind; love is not jealous, or conceited, or proud; love is not ill-mannered, or selfish, or irritable; love does not keep a record of wrongs; love is not happy with evil, but is happy with the truth. Love never gives up: its faith, hope, and patience never fail."

Then Father MacSween pushed himself out of the padded chair, and limped to the pulpit. He wiped his brow with the handkerchief and stuck it back into his cassock, looked as though he wasn't sure what he was doing at the front of the church.

"I asked Father Gillis what I should talk about," he said, looking momentarily uncertain. "He told me to begin at the beginning." Father MacSween smiled the pained smile that I remembered from the days we were friends. Life is hard, but kindness abides, the smile said.   He brightened as though the solution had just occurred to him.

"So I'll begin with the first human thing. The first human thing is sin. Sin is what we humans do. Sin is what we're all about. Marriage is the hardest thing in the world. People who get married are very brave," Father MacSween continued. "If they knew all that I know, they'd be afraid to do it. That's one reason I'm a priest."

He lowered his eyes, and shook his head again, waiting for the ripple of laughter to subside.

"Marriage has everything against it. For two people to work and live together their whole life, share everything, remain true to each other, it's almost impossible..."

A baby on the groom's side of the church began to cry; someone coughed. Father MacSween, in no hurry, stopped. He waited until everyone was looking at him again.

"Almost impossible... It's against human nature. Every parish priest knows this. It's against our natures, which, because of original sin, means that we always fail to be as good as we want to be. The trouble is the world is against marriage, and human nature is against marriage." Again, the pensive and slow shake of his head. "People try, though. They try anyway. People want to be good. People want to love each other as Christ tells us to do."

Father MacSween reached into his cassock, extracted his white handkerchief, touched it to his forehead, and replaced it.

"For most people, if they are going to save themselves, it will be in marriage."

"We only need to hear the words from the gospel, and we know they are true. We know what we are supposed to do. You don't need a priest to tell you those words are true. 'Love is patient and kind; love seeks not itself to please.' I look at the bride and groom today, and I see two people who love each other, and I see two people who will try to love as Christ tells us to love. But I say to them, what I said to their parents when I married them thirty years ago, and what I said to some of the rest of you sitting in this church today. Life is hard, and marriage is one of the hardest things in life.

"That is why the Church calls it a sacrament, and it is one of the hardest sacraments to practice. So much is asked of men and women in marriage. And there are so many distractions, so much that invites men and women to betray each other, to go against their vows, to forget or put aside the truths they know so deeply on their wedding day. Original sin makes us want to not live up to our vows, to betray each other. Some few will help each other and not look back. Others will fall and get up and go from there. Others will fail and give up.

"That is why we have two priests up here at the altar today. That's why we played the bagpipes and also the organ, and that is why all our friends and families have joined us. That's why we'll have a dance tonight with singing and laughter and shouting, and the best food and drink, and the finest band the people who love you can afford.

"We want to try to help the two of you to succeed at this difficult thing you have decided to try to do."

Again, Father MacSween extracted his white hankerchief from his cassock, and slowly wiped sweat from his forehead and his pallid face. Then he returned the handkerchief to his cassock. When he resumed, his voice was more confiding, more effective for the obvious effort his words were costing him.. "Because we're older than you, and have lived longer than you, and have made mistakes you haven't made, we know things you can't know yet. We also know that we can't be as much help as we'd like to be. We can't do much. We can't stop sin, and we can't take original sin away from you or from anybody else. Maybe it helps, a little, when we here today tell you that we wish the best for you, for that baby that you all love so much.

Father MacSween inhaled, gathered himself up, smiled his sad smile once more, and limped back to his padded seat at the back of the altar.

After the service, we stepped outside, walked across the gravel parking lot to the receiving line at the edge of the parking lot. The village of St. Andrews — a fork in the road, a credit union in a house trailer, a Co-op store, a school, and two dozen houses — sprawled beneath us. I hugged the mother of the bride, shook hands with my former friend the father-of-the-bride, hugged the bride, my former student, and stepped around Father MacSween, who was seated in a chair and therefore avoidable.

We didn't go to the reception. It was the MacSweenites night to be joyous. They didn't need me there complicating their communal good feeling.

In the months that followed, I saw less of him but heard reports about his health. Avoiding him at the reception, I realized, had been a missed opportunity. The way he was built and the way I was built, I wasn't going to go and talk to him. Then, one October morning, I heard he was dead. Heart attack, coming back from Cape Breton, no pain. I'd never get things right with him, never even have the consolation of knowing I'd done my bit.

Where Father MacSween is now, he'll feel no regret or joy in anything I or anyone else have to say about him. I'd like to try to tell as much of the truth as I can face. *De mortuis nihil nise bonum*, as that generation of Catholics would have it. This story is about pride, mine mostly, but Father MacSween's, too.

At the funeral I sat in the back of the Church, like a judge, as people I'd once loved, people with problems in their lives, problems like mine only, in most cases bigger, people who don't tell lies very often, tend to care about the things I care about, who share their blessings, help each other and might be glad to help me again. Why am I a person who will walk across the street not to talk to them? What if, several turns back, I made a wrong turn?

In January 1974, I came to St. F.X. for a job interview. The English Department needed an Americanist. I was an American, a Catholic, and I had a personal connection with one of his former students who was on the faculty. At my visit I was shepherded by the usual aggregate of department chair and faculty members. We came to Father MacSween's office, I was introduced to him. I was struck by how big he was, then by how soft his hand was when I shook it (I've since got used to professors's soft hands; I have pretty soft hands myself).

"Phil talks to Johnny today," the Chairman said.

John Sears was the Dean of Arts via the Business faculty. His reputation was as out-sized as Father MacSween's. A couple of weeks before my interview, he had been quoted by the student newspaper.

"You could fire a cannon down the hallway on the fourth floor of Nicholson Hall any time after three in the

afternoon and not worry about hitting anyone," the
Xaverian Weekly quoted him as saying.

"Ph. D.'s in English are a dime a dozen," was the
quote my colleagues-to-be attributed to him that day. I
don't remember what Father MacSween said. The
sentiment must have been, Good Luck. You'll need it.
Whatever he said, everyone broke up laughing.

The next September I joined the St. F.X. English
faculty. Our offices were both on the north side of
Nicholson Hall, on either side of the elevator shaft, overlooking the Cathedral and the mountain.

He'd stick his head in my office.

"Had your coffee yet?" became his usual greeting.

I'd stop what I was doing, and up we'd go to the
coffee lounge. He seemed to float, as though he weren't
connected to his body, as he walked to the elevator, across
the lounge to the coffee pots. Then nodding and smiling
his embarrassed smile, he'd negotiate the forty yards across
the huge lounge to his big chair by the window at the far
end. I still think of that area as the MacSween Corner.

Students nicknamed him "Moonbeam." With his
huge face, and pained smile, and this disembodied quality,
the name seemed to me to fit him like a glove. But I
quickly learned that he detested the name. It turned out
that "Moonbeam MacSwine" was a character in the *Li'l
Abner* cartoon strip, who had never taken a bath. I assume
now that someone from a coal mining town would not want
a nickname with such associations.

Father MacSween taught twelve or fifteen hours a
week, including a required religion course, for much of his
career. He served as chaplain to the sisters at the Mount.
He tried to perform what must have been the impossible

job of running a residence hall in days when alcohol was forbidden, carnality was vigilantly suppressed, and lights went out at 10:30 p.m. so students could get their required sleep.   One student who lived in residence in the 1960s expressed admiration for his ability to keep order without getting worked up over small breaches of the rules. Father MacSween prefected as though he knew life had more important things in it than rules, things such as T. S. Eliot's poems and saying something witty.   Father MacSween could forgive a lot of a person who could make him smile.

I knew him only near the end of his career, when circumstances finally permitted him to live the intellectual life he must always have felt he was intended to lead. He taught one course, edited the *Antigonish Review*, and wrote poems and stories. After I was here a short time, he gave up the course. A couple years later, he turned the review over to his former students.

He wore a navy blue nylon jacket, with crossed hockey sticks. "ST. F.X. HOCKEY," it proclaimed in white letters over the heart. If I or one of his former students didn't join him, he sat alone and read from the *Sewanee Review* or *Encounter* that he always carried with him.

Our conversations followed a pattern.   He introduced a topic. If I knew something about it, I told him what I knew, and we passed on to the next topic or the next one until we found a topic that I didn't know about. I would say, I don't know Russian history. Or, I don't know that. Or, I'm afraid I haven't read any George Moore. Then he would enlighten me. He would give me a summary of Moore's life, then begin on his major works, judging each one as he summarized the plot for me. Thus, I learned the plots of novels, about poems I wanted to read, especially about the lives of authors.

He believed truth was absolute. Certainty on all issues was achievable. Once he'd achieved it, it was true for him and for everyone else. There would be no further discussion. If he'd concluded a colleague was evil or a fool, he expected me to agree with his judgement. If he didn't like a writer's work, then that writer couldn't be worth my time. This could extend to the smallest matters.

I also learned I was not to disagree with him. Once he told me Minnie Minoso was a Chicago Cub.

"No, Minnie played for the White Sox. I'm sure," I added. "I grew up listening to the White Sox games on radio."

"Minoso was a Cub," Father repeated.

"It doesn't matter," I said.

He gave me his hard look.

"You're disagreeing with me," he said. Then he smiled his pained smile.

His knowledge of T. S. Eliot and Ezra Pound was as broad as anyone's I have ever met. We shared an enthusiasm for American writing of the early twentieth century that extended to such minor writers as the brothers Binet, John Peale Bishop, Edna St. Vincent Millay, Edgar Lee Masters, Ellen Glasgow, and others. I was probably the only person he knew that could have carried on a discussion about some of these writers with him. But once he'd determine I knew a writer's work, he'd turn the conversation to another one, whom I wouldn't know about, and he'd tell me about that one.

He was never able to relate to me (or, from what I have seen, to his students) as other than priest, mentor, confessor. If ever a human being was imprisoned by his mythology it was Father MacSween. His reputation as the best read man in Canada, great poet, novelist, and short story writer, hilarious conversationalist, *the* priest who maintains the dignity of his vocation, great professor, brilliant editor, handwriting expert_along with all his community's expectations that went with his priestly status_must have locked him into an immense cage from which there was to be no escape.

I still quote Father MacSween when I teach Frost's "Two Tramps at Mudtime." The two tramps come and see the narrator splitting wood. He's splitting oak for firewood (that dates the poem), and he is loving it. He tells how far apart his feet are when he addresses the stove lengths, how the logs split neatly in two when he hits them. It is an April day, summer when the sun is out, and February again when it disappears behind a cloud. Frost is hitting the wood just right, when the tramps approach. He ends up letting the tramps split the wood because they need the money.

"Frost is boasting," Father said.

"Boasting?" I said.

"Yes, about how good he is at splitting wood, about having money, about being a poet."

I don't say Father MacSween was right or wrong when I teach that poem. I tell my students what he told me. "Well, was Father MacSween right? Is Frost bragging?" I ask, as the soul of Father MacSween looks down. It seemed a strange tack to take on the poem to me then. Now, I consider it Maritime Canadian. A person doesn't want to be caught posturing. One keeps one's eye open for other people posturing.

"Come to lunch with me?" he'd ask as though I would be doing him a favour. He always waited until after 12:45 or so. I'd clear a space to sit among the books on the front seat of his Pontiac, buckle up, and Father MacSween would back out of his spot beside the basement door of Nicholson, turn and pass Bloomfield, drive around past liquor lane, MacIsaac, the Coady Institute, and the Oland Centre, round the corner past the football fields, up past the maintenance shack, and park the car in front of the dining hall. It was a mile and a half drive taken to save us a 300 yard walk. If another priest came in, he might join us, but usually the dining room was empty except for us and the student-waiter.

How I ate at those lunches. A tray of salads, a fish course, a meat course, three kinds of bread, and several desserts, served by handsome young boys who stood there in uniform, anticipating our desire for seconds or dessert or refills.

Our discussions were less literary than our coffee room ones. We'd discuss Cape Breton, interesting people he had known, the Church, and university life as he remembered it. Here, Father MacSween listened to what I had to say.

When I have been with Father MacSween and his students, I have always had a hilarious time. People expected Father MacSween to say funny things, and they laughed when he said them. Some wine or beer, then jokes, laughs, funny stories, more laughs, more jokes and stories and laughs. The kind of laugh I like least is where the truth is stretched to make a joke, where everyone becomes one of E.M. Forster's flat characters, this person a function of his tightness with money, that one a function of his sexuality, that one of the prissy way she clears her throat before speaking.   When I was with Father MacSween and his students it was mostly the latter kind of jokes that we laughed at until tears came. The ultimate condemnation was that someone lacked a sense of humour.

Alone with him in the priest's dining hall, I saw a quieter wit.   The characters in his stories were more complicated, their foibles as likely to be endearing or pathetic as funny, their vices sad.   He favoured verbal twists that illuminated small truths.   Nothing was exaggerated for comic effect. Though spontaneous humour wasn't my strong suit, he showed me how to savour certain of life's sad and funny ironies in a way I'd not have found if left to my own devices.

The best insights of the thoughtful man I knew never made it into the things he wrote. I think he liked me, but he never trusted me or himself enough to let me see his frailty. His writing voice, too, is that of a mentor, priest, and teacher.

"Out of my quarrel with my friends, I make rhetoric.   Out of my quarrel with myself, I make literature," Yeats is said to have said. Neither quarrel makes it into Father MacSween's writing. The things he wrestled with in his life hardly appear. When they do appear, mostly in his poems, he presents the conclusion, not the process of his wrestling.

You would hardly guess, reading him, that he lived in Nova Scotia all his life. His fiction seems set in some unnamed and non-descript American city.[1] Partly, this was out of kindness to those he knew. He refused, on principle, to write anything that might cause pain.

But this was in his writing. In his personal life, he didn't spare other people's feelings. Those who knew him tell of devastating put downs he dropped on people, of his formidableness at meetings, of his ability to humiliate those he found foolish or pretentious. I still consider some people to be fools based mostly on stories Father MacSween told me about them. He was a great hater, and I was lucky not to have earned his hatred until he was old and was turning his thoughts to more important things than earthly feuds.

Father MacSween was a lonely man who spent a lot of time thinking about the big questions of life and death, loneliness, and the meaning of it all. His poetry comes closer to dealing with the material of his life than his fiction. His best poems offer honest conclusions that emerge from a lifetime of thinking. He deals thoughtfully with important questions, but he is never candid, never risks failure, never delves into the stickier aspects of experience. He wrote for people he knew, he said.

His poetry is the poetry of a well read man who is thinking about life. He loved Pound, but he didn't aspire

----

[1]There is an exception. *Furiously Wrinkled* is a novel based on something that happened in Glace Bay, which I think he wrote after noting the success two of his former students found in Cape Breton material that Father MacSween knew at least as well as they did. But *Furiously Wrinkled* is a tired book, and when Father MacSween's former students came out with their memorial volume, they didn't include anything from it.

to the clarity of image that Pound achieved.   He
embroiders ideas together on his reading, on loneliness, on
his observations of the life around him.

In his reviews and criticism, where the voice of the
mentor is natural, he does not seem to be speaking to
people he knows at all. No matter who he was writing for
— the readers of an alumni magazine, the *Scotia Sun*, or
the tiny international audience he addressed in his literary
magazine — the criticism seems to be written for some
fellow omnivorous reader who has read all the books he
read. He is contributing to a debate that goes on in the
pages of *TLS*, the *New York* Times Book Review, and
Encounter. The criticism and reviews tend to be concerned
with the precise measurement of the accomplishment of
prominent writers, distinguishing between the excellent and
the not-quite-so-good.

The critical essays the editors include are on
Alexander Pope, Cardinal Newman, Graham Greene,
McLuhan, Eliade, Chesterton, Waugh, Hemingway,
Pound, Lawrence and Father Hopkins. Newman, Pope,
Chesterton, Waugh, and Greene were all Catholic. Even
Hemingway was Catholic for a while.   Only D. H.
Lawrence and Ezra Pound, among non-Catholics, were
chosen for critical attention.

"As I get older, people seem so trivial to me," he
told me once at coffee. "My writing isn't for them any
more. I write only for God now."

I pictured God, up there in heaven, reading one of
Father MacSween's novels. I should have known that I
was in the presence of an exceptional man. I don't know
who I write for — for the professorati too much of the time
— but one could do worse than to write for God.

He did not write at all for the usual Canadian literary magazine audience. He truly didn't know or care what was going on with his fellow editors of little magazines and the people who published poems in those magazines. Certainly, he could have been an *ex officio* member of that club, one of those "internationally famous in Canada" writers who give readings, have their books reviewed, and are considered important because they are at the centre of the little storm. I saw baffled writer/editors of other reviews more or less offer to get his work praised. He loved praise, but he was a mile above that particular form of fraud.[2]

About ten years before he died, he decided to get rid of his books. He invited me to his room at MacIsaac. To visit Father MacSween's rooms was to enter a rickety

---

[2]Fraudulence and pride are a professor's occupational hazards. Students, administrators, politicians, and taxpayers all have a vested interest in concluding that university faculty members are geniuses. And we *are*, every one of us, foremost experts in something, even if it is only how many times lions are mentioned in King Henry IV, or the number of spots on the dorsal fin of a Middleton Lake ocean trout.

Father MacSween, for the most part refused to play the genius game. Once, when Moses Coady was still alive and was hosting a visiting dignitary from the Carnegie Foundation in New York City, Father MacSween was making his solitary way across the priest's dining hall.

"See that man there," Moses Coady said to the New York dignitary. "That's the best read man in Canada."

I think Father MacSween felt that he merited that compliment. Beyond that, he seemed uncomfortable with the claims others made on his behalf.

shrine to learning. There was not a plant or living thing in his rooms except Father MacSween himself. The university carpenters had put bookshelves everywhere, from floor to ceiling. Books upright from end to end, and then on top of them were books horizontal. The headboard of his bed was stacked with books, as was the kitchen table. His television set was piled high with them, and they were under and on top of his end tables. The floor was covered with books. That was the part I saw. I think he'd moved the books he most cherished into his bed room, where I didn't go.

"Help yourself," he said to me. "Take whatever you want."

I took a small stack of books, and thanked him.

"No, you don't understand, Phil. I want to get rid of them. Take whatever you want. There are some boxes in the kitchen. I protested once more, then loaded two large soap boxes with books. A week later I returned with my emptied boxes and filled them again.

The books I took I still use. Many of them I cherish, and when I open them, I find his name, R. J. MacSween, and all that marginalia. He underlined epigrammatic statements that he agreed with. He also underlined and wrote notes in the margins about statements that offered empirical evidence for the existence of God or the truth of Roman Catholicism. He debated, in the margins, the contentious points. He corrected grammar. Many paragraphs received exclamation marks; others, he refuted.

These were not social calls. Father MacSween didn't put the kettle on. We chatted, briefly, mostly about individual books, and his judgement on them and their authors. He cared about books. He had friends he liked better than he liked me, but he thought I was a person who would appreciate the books. It was an objective compliment he was paying me, and its significance has been lost on me until now.

Things that I did ultimately drove him into voluntary exile from the English Department and the university. I usually think of myself as on the side of the angels in this. Here, I will try to give Father MacSween his due. The English Department, which had lost several members without hiring anybody in the ten years after I was hired, was given permission to hire somebody. Father MacSween had been retired for several years, but there he was, planning to attend his first English Department meeting in years, championing a former student for the job. A friend and I hatched a motion (a motion we had lined up votes for) that the search committee should consist of all full-time faculty. We knew, of course, that without Father MacSween voting, the department would look seriously at all the candidates, and that his candidate would probably not be hired.

Shortly before our falling out, in one of our priest's dining room conversations, Father MacSween told me this.

"Burton MacDonald said to me once, 'Father, you've had a long and full life. What do you most regret?'" Father MacSween looked at me, and waited.

"Big question," I said.

"I told him the thing I most regret is all the times I made a fool of myself," he said. "That's what I remember now, all the foolish things I've done."

He'd called in all his chips. His former students, the priestly establishment, nobody could prevent his public

humiliation.   When it must have looked to Father
MacSween like outsiders who didn't value much of
anything except their academic specialties were taking
over, I revealed myself as one more foreign Ph.D. with a
bloodless agenda.

After Eve ate the apple that contained knowledge of
good and evil, and brought sin into the world, Milton says,
"Earth felt the wound." That is what I thought of when I
made my little move. All sorts of people stopped speaking.
The Chair of the English Department (my truer mentor)
took a heart attack. Suddenly, there were rooms I was no
longer welcome in. The dean sent an angry letter. Priests
began to glare at me (Some of this might have been in my
head).   The hilarity that marked his former students'
conversations ended when I came in the room.   My
association with the *Antigonish Review* ended.

Weaned on Republic studio westerns, the righteous
posture of Gary Cooper in *High Noon* is the one I am most
comfortable with. The more difficult my life became, the
more former and fair-weather friends I gained, the more
certain I was that I was right. I wanted a better English
Department. I fought for the process that I felt would
make a proper department.

But professionalism, I've learned since, has traps,
too. I did not realize how quickly the incestuous old guard
would disappear, how quickly ambitious outsiders would
become the rule.   "Academic Incest" or "in-breeding"
seemed to be the enemy.

But a small rural university can find itself with a
collection of careerists who were not hired by the more
prominent universities they would have chosen. The best

of these people "publish their way out," but many of them
are stuck.

There is no such neat word as "in-breeding" to
describe a university full of ambitious outsiders who cannot
publish their way out. At the time I could not imagine a
faculty of academics whose contempt for the eastern Nova
Scotia ethos was exceeded only by their ignorance of it.

But that soon became other people's problem. My
quarrel with Father MacSween and his students came at the
apex of my career as a mover and shaker. I soon dropped
out. I did not have the stomach for it.

Nowadays, I issue Jeremiads and screeds. I send
screaming memos, make passionate speeches that cause
others to smile behind their hands. I command an army of
one, and my appeals for recruits have not been successful.

What have you done for me lately? was my posture
toward the *Antigonish Review* in the days I was involved in
it. I never stopped to think what a miracle it was that it
existed at all.

The arty, the literary, and the impractical are
distrusted here on principle. Father MacSween overcame
what must have been profound opposition. He must have
raised money, steered his project through an early version
of St. F.X.'s complicated committee structure, and got
support from unlikely places. Probably, nobody could
have launched and maintained a serious literary review at
St. F.X. except the man who did it.

He published only what he considered to be the best
of the submissions he received. Famous Canadian poet or
St. F. X. Pooh Bah, it didn't matter. Their poems were
turned down if they didn't fit Father MacSween's sense of
what belonged in his *Review*. More than once, in my early

days, I was invited by a rejected author to agree that Father's taste was fallible. More than once, a local reader asked me to look at something Father MacSween had published in his *Review* — a poem about masturbation, a graphic description of sex, a poem or story with a four letter word — and agree that it was shameless, garbage, filth; that MacSween (a priest no less!) had crossed the line between literary expression and pornography.

Nowadays, we St. F.X. professors obsessively tally how many of our students get into graduate programs, and cite these statistics to prove we are doing a good job. I suspect none of us can claim as much as Father MacSween could have claimed had he cared to count. At least five of his former students holding Ph.D.'s are teaching English or philosophy at St. F.X. Another former student, also with a Ph.D., might be the best writer of fiction in Canada. Others, I occasionally hear about, teach English at other Canadian universities.

There are many ways to be a great professor. Most professors do not discover any of them. I suspect Father MacSween found the only way that an omnivorous reader and priest from Cape Breton who loves to read becomes a great English professor.

He required students to keep a journal or scrapbook, in which they pasted pictures they'd clipped from magazines to illustrate the poems and stories they read. I remember pictures of sunsets, and quotes from poems about the beauty of nature. I dismissed his scrapbooks as high school. A few years ago, I began my own experiment with journals. Last year, I invited a published poet to give my creative writing students some advice. She showed my class her journal. It was full of pictures: here a nice sunset, there a picture of her mother on her wedding day, there an aphorism or couplet she'd come across in a magazine. It looked like one of Father MacSween's student scrapbooks.

Father MacSween was a full professor with a B.A. degree. At least three students in different years told me versions of this story. St. F.X. wanted him to get a Ph.D. in English, so they insisted he go to Catholic University in Washington, D.C. Father MacSween stayed there for a month, and was doing very well when the Chair of the English Department called him into his office.

"Look," the Chair said. "We don't feel qualified to teach you. You've read all the books, and you know everything we know. We think you should go home."

Anybody who has done graduate studies in English knows that there does not exist a student intellect so formidable that a graduate program in English cannot bully and cajole it into surrender without questioning its assumptions for a fraction of a second.

All that is left of Father MacSween is his writing and his editing. This is unfortunate, because he was a priest, a teacher, a reader and bibliophile, a loyal St. F.X.er, and a friend before he was either a writer or an editor.

His love of books is rightly legendary. He loved them so much he could recognize them by their colours and shapes, by the graphics on the covers, by their thickness and height. He worried that they wouldn't survive the library's transition from the Dewey decimal system to the Library of Congress classification.

I recently looked at six old black and white pictures of Father MacSween. Five are of a man I never knew:

thin and dark haired with no more sadness in his face than anybody else has. The man I knew was a different person. I cannot put the two faces together. I'd like to have known the man in the pictures, a priest with a thin and undefeated face organizing a group of girl guides in the 1940s, standing at an anvil and captain's wheel (in a coal mine?) a few years later, and reading a book in Mockler Hall in 1955. This must have been the Father MacSween who taught my colleagues. But in their reminiscences, certainly in Bill Mitchell's loving portrait, his former students describe the sad-faced giant I knew.

The last picture, taken in 1981, shows Father MacSween with his former students. "Editorial Board, Spring 1981," the caption says. The editors, my colleagues, stand in a half circle behind Father MacSween, whose look says that he has better things to do than have his picture taken. Bill Mitchell looks down. Richard Leader and Michael Stubbs and Wendell Gillies have nearly identical expressions, as though something terrible looms behind the photographer. Only Mary Leader bothers to smile, and her smile is fading as the picture is snapped.

The Father MacSween they love lives in people's minds. Theirs especially, but also in the minds of people like myself who crossed him, but who, for better or worse, are the teachers and writers and people they are, partly because they had his solid presence to define themselves against.

In spite of too many classes and students to teach, too many masses to conduct, too much time spent as a cop in residence halls, too much time working at the corrupting business of running a university department, and what must have been a numbing life as a priest in the Church's age of contraction, Father MacSween led a life in literature. He looked for the best and the truest and the most beautiful in writing. When given a chance, late in his life, to write and to edit a journal, he turned out a large amount of poetry, a novel, short stories, and a lot of criticism in a short time. That the editors of the *Antigonish Review* rank it higher than I do is hardly the point. He respected writing too much to hustle or play games with it. He never forgot that thousands of great writers wrote before him. In his *Review*, he sought to publish the best writing that came in over his transom, and to encourage the most promising writers who passed through his classes or who came to Antigonish to meet him.

The next time I saw him I was standing in front of his casket on a warm October morning. He'd taken a heart attack driving back from Cape Breton. I've tried to do him and myself the justice of telling as much of the truth as I can face. I was secretive and manipulative in the way I handled that hiring so long ago, and in other ways, too.

I had reached the point where I no longer spoke to my colleagues and former friends. I marked the evidence of mortality in their worry lines, grey hair, balding heads, and middle-aged paunches, as they bore the stern and pleasant duties of being Father MacSween's friends for the last time. Michael and Richard read from the *Bible*, Wendell did the intercessions, Bill and Stewart helped carry the coffin.

It was a measure of my alienation that I didn't march in the academic procession. It would have been hypocritical. Still, I felt like a coward back there in the second row from the back.

They believed in kindness, cherished the salt of human personality; and like their master, they saw humour as a mildly effective palliative to the pain that life lays on us all. All I can do now is set the record as straight as I can set it. I can also promise myself to try to set a few other things as straight as I can set them, too. He didn't live to see me try to set the record straight. He was blocked in his life by at least as much complicating pride as I am blocked in mine. But I think he would understand. Sin, he said at the wedding, is the first human thing.

Winter

The Professor Lectures His Neighbor

I'm sorry you fell into Hector MacDonald's ditch
and broke the headlight on your motorcycle, Elroy. And
I'm sorry Jiggs chased you.   Here is my cheque for
$94.12. It is exactly the amount Netta-san told me on the
phone she thought I should pay you. Ninety-four dollars
and twelve cents seems like a lot of money for a headlight.
But, this being Antigonish, and you being a neighbour, we
both know I can't afford not to pay.

It is no secret that Jiggs is not an intelligent dog.
He house broke easily enough, but we have never been
able to teach him not to bring home the esophagi, bladders,
hoofs, and intestines that your father strews along the river
bank, thinking he's feeding the eagles and ospreys, after he
and his drinking buddies butcher their deer every autumn.
Jiggs brings them into our yard, chews them for a while,
and leaves them for the snow to bury. You, too, must
have smiled when you saw my too-fastidious kids, in the
springtime mud, noses pinched shut with gloved fingers,
scooping up deer innards with rakes and long-handled
shovels, and dropping them into a garbage bag.

When Jiggs hears pebbles clatter against
undercoating, his head goes up, his ears go back, and he is
off — growling, barking, seeking to bite a tire. He returns

with his head and tail high. He thinks he has performed a valuable service.

What can I do? I tried shouting at him, hitting him with a rolled newspaper, locked him in the shed. My wife took him to dog obedience school at the arena one winter. Every Wednesday evening for six weeks. Jiggs learned to heel, to stay, and to lie down on his stomach, to roll over, even to shake hands. But one look at you on your Yamaha, Elroy, and all of this expensive learning goes right out the window.

The dog obedience instructor suggested that we borrow a car, and get Jiggs to chase it, then slam on the brakes, and chase Jiggs.

"Sometimes, that'll work," he said. But he wasn't hopeful. "Chasers tend to be chasers," he added. "There's not much you can do."

As I told your mother on the phone, Elroy, Jiggs would have been gone long ago if the decision had been mine. Jiggs has been there most of my son's life. But good relations inside a family are even more important than good relations with neighbors.

You probably don't know this, but the day you threw that folding chair off the back of a pickup truck at Jiggs a couple of years ago, my son and one of his sisters were watching. My son wanted me to go back there and punch you in the nose. In fact, this evening, before my wife sent me over with this check, we talked about you and Jiggs, and I learned a few things about you and Jiggs. According to my kids, you have thrown at least one water balloon and several stones at him, kicked at him countless times, opened Rod J's car door on ·his charging body dozens of times.

I had hoped the whole thing would blow over, that I'd lend your mum our apple juicer, give her some of our crabapple jelly, a few litres of July honey, and then your father and I would have a glass of rum and talk about the weather, that you'd gradually stop seething.

My son said that he saw you in the hallway at school today — you in your black jacket, the helmet under your arm, holding your unfamiliar pink scribbler in your large hand.

"I'm going to kill Jiggs," my son said you said.

"You do and I'll burn your house down," my son said he replied to you.

"Did Elroy smile?" I asked my son.

"Elroy didn't smile and I didn't smile," my son said.

Now that we're talking fire and death, I'd like to suggest we approach this from another direction. I never thought Jiggs — who has been hit by cars six times that we know of and who still persists in crossing the Trans-Canada Highway in search of garbage cans, — would live so long.

And, if I may be frank, Elroy, your behavior puzzles me. I've seen you bait a muskrat trap, fix a carburetor, shoot a squirrel out of a tree, snare an ocean trout, and do a dozen other difficult things I wish I could do. *Your* intelligence, unlike Jiggs', isn't an issue here.

When you went into that ditch, you could have been killed or maimed. Your three thousand dollar motorcycle could have been totalled. I can afford $94.12 once. But I can't afford to buy you a new bike. To save three thousand dollars I will endure some icy relationships with neighbours.

You must have noticed that Jiggs doesn't chase your brother Henry, who drives slowly. I'm suggesting a new tactic. My suggestion is that you pet Jiggs once or twice, that you not kick him as you blast past on your Yamaha, that you maybe stop, get off your bike, and hand Jiggs one of the dog biscuits I am anxious to provide you with. One of Jiggs' virtues, after all, is that he never met a pedestrian he didn't like. When he knows and likes the person under the helmet, he doesn't chase.

I think its worth a try, Elroy.

5   "some private business"

In most books, the I, or first person, is omitted; in this it will be retained; that, in respect to egotism, is the main difference. We commonly do not remember that it is, after all, always the first person that is speaking. I should not talk so much about myself if there were anybody else whom I knew as well. Unfortunately, I am confined to this theme by the narrowness of my experience.

— Henry David Thoreau, *Walden*

The wind blew cold from Malignant Cove. It was minus seventeen. Every face looked pasty, glum, worried, self-absorbed. The flag on top of Nicholson was a tattered reddish rag. Old professors became testier, more suspicious, more self absorbed. Young ones eyed the graveyard across the Trans-Canada, and scanned (once more) the ads in *University Affairs*. Memos from Deans and ambitious chairs took on a sniping tone.

Students picked their way to class along paths cleared through the snow, which was banked high wherever there was room to pile it. Students who'd arrived healthy and tanned in September looked grey and blotchy and defeated after three months of late hours, and dining hall stew.

It was, in short, February, that long dead roll from Christmas until March without a holiday. It was exactly the time to be somewhere else. I and ten of the students in my Puritans and Transcendentalists course were heading to Boston. We'd spent September through December studying

Henry David Thoreau, Nathaniel Hawthorne, Margaret Fuller, Walt Whitman, and Ralph Waldo Emerson. What could be better than to visit the very place Thoreau undertook his great experiment at Walden, where Hawthorne wrote *The Scarlet Letter*, and Margaret Fuller edited *The Dial*? An 800 mile drop down the coast looked easy.

At Christmas one of the three serious students phoned with the news he was quitting school. He would drive a truck or bus plates during the day, and take a single university course at night. He'd learn more that way, he said.

I pointed out to the second of my three serious students that her paper on Thoreau, though it had good things in it, seemed over-written, out of touch with her perceptions. In a burst of wounded righteousness, she, too, dropped the course.

I was down to one student who actually wanted the best I had to give on the literature I cared most about.

But there were others in the class: a phys-edder who possessed a cheerful certainty that he already knew all the world's unsilly ideas, two pretty coeds from the West who leaked lovely puffs of lilac and sandalwood into the seminar room whenever they turned in their chairs,[1] an eighteen-hour-a-day student union politician who scurried through the nearest door when she saw me at the SUB; an American with the sullen righteousness of a hanging judge; a nice girl from Cape Breton who wasn't sure whether she was more terrified of me or my subject; and an affable political science major who came most alive when

---

[1] I thought of them as the Duelling Blowdryers.

explaining why the nice guys at MacIsaac Hall didn't deserve their vile reputation.

I cadged $250 from the English department budget, got another $200 from the alumni office in return for a promise of usable copy[2], invited myself and my students to the house of a friend from my Notre Dame days who lived near Boston.   And gloated.   Never would seven people go so far (1900 miles) for so long (4 days) on so little ($450.00 and my winning smile).

It was drizzling wet snow, an inch of slush on the ground, when we set out for Concord.   It was the first snow Boston had had that winter.   The ranger, in a kiosk on the road, said it was an easy half mile walk.

We crossed the road on foot, and descended the path.   Two ice fishermen were on the pond, and some crows watched us from the oak trees, which dropped dry brown leaves onto the snow. We walked along the white path, following the occasional sign, looking for Thoreau's cabin.

The wind was raw and cold, snow was wet and heavy, the sky like slate.   Though the temperature was barely freezing, the students were chilled.   They had not expected, in spite of all the promises in my pedagogy, to be outdoors.   The snow gave way to drizzling rain.

---

[2]There had been a time, and not that long before the adventure here recounted, when the publication of things I wrote did not inspire nervous tremours, de-fusing, and spin doctoring from those charged with making the world outside the campus think other of our university, its teachers, and students than the facts would entitle the world to think of them.

"How much farther is it?" one of the Duelling Blowdryers asked.

"It can't be much farther," I said. "Why?"

"My feet are so cold," she said.

"Well, it can't be far."

"I'm cold, too," her friend said, and she had wrapped her cloak around her neck.

Our phys-edder, with his exuberant athleticism, scampered ahead, seeking Thoreau's cabin. He seemed to be the only student besides me who was up to this trip.

A hundred yards later, I heard my name being called. I walked to where they were standing.

"Yes?"

"I can't go on," my student said. I heard her teeth chattering. "I'm chilled. I'm sorry. These boots aren't very warm."

She was wearing boots with a two-inch high heel that disappeared under her coat. They *looked* warm, but her teeth were chattering, and there was a tear running down her face.

"Well, you'd better go back," I said.

I gave her the keys to my car, so she could turn on the heater.

"Should I go with her, Dr. Milner?" her friend asked.

"Do what you think you should do," I replied, curious about what she would say.

"I think I'd better go."

The two of them retreated down the path toward my car, and the faithful remnant pushed on to the site of Thoreau's cabin. Each time the path turned, I expected to see the outline of the shack, or the cairn that Bronson

Alcott started for Thoreau. But we didn't see it for a long time.

The pond without people was lovely, but I felt only the weight of my visibly suffering students. Today, I could only look back at my little platoon who wished they were home.

Finally, I saw a sign with words and an arrow:

CABIN SITE
→

Then we came to the cairn and the outline of the cabin. Like victorious mountain climbers, we decided to take a picture to commemorate our accomplishment. I still have that picture. I'm looking at it as I write. We sullenly froze into unnatural poses, each student throwing a stone on the cairn as the camera snapped.

We'd gone to visit the place in the world where an experiment in living took place. Thoreau had set out to see if a person could live joyously and spontaneously, with little money, in the middle of a woods. We had blown all the money we could lay hands on, dressed in fashionable and expensive clothes that did not keep us warm, and gone to the middle of the woods that Thoreau happily did without in.

A huge rock pile, called a cairn by the explanatory sign that invited pilgrims to contribute their rocks, stood beside the cabin.

"One. Two. Three. Drop them!" someone called.

We dropped our stones in unison. The camera clicked. The moment has been preserved on film. One student held his ankle with one hand, and dropped his stone with the other. We smiled like people smile at a camera after they've caught a giant fish.

"The man who goes alone can start today; but he who travels with another must wait till that other is ready," Thoreau wrote in *Walden*. Thoreau would not have juggled the system to make a trip for people who didn't truly want the trip.

Thoreau lived alone in the woods at Walden Pond for two years, conducting what he called an economic experiment. He fished the pond, kept a garden, maintained his shack, and took odd jobs. "I am rich according to the number of things I can do without," he wrote. He discovered that if he worked six weeks a year as a labourer, he had all the money he needed. "We are for the most part more lonely when we go abroad among men than when we stay in our chambers. A man thinking or working is always alone, let him be where he will."

Emerson smiled at his cantankerousness; publishers turned his books down, and hardly anyone showed up for his public lectures. At the end of *Walden*, he boasted: "If one advances confidently in the direction of his dreams, and endeavors to live the life which he has imagined, he will meet with a success unexpected in common hours." He considered himself a great success.

From Walden, we went to Bronson Alcott's house and the Transcendental School. The school combined the less happy features of a church and a barn. Alcott lost most of his students when parents realized that his airy ideas had implications. The family was saved from financial ruin by Alcott's daughter, Louisa May, who wrote the best-selling *Little Women*. Our visit provided my remaining serious student with a senior thesis topic, and, perhaps, an area of specialization for her graduate study. Sleepy Hollow Cemetery, our last stop, had elaborate gravestones and Authors Ridge, where the writers were buried. I asked the cheerful physical education major to read Longfellow's poem on Hawthorne's burial. His classmates giggled in discomfort. He didn't understand the poem, didn't want to understand it.

The next day, we put ourselves into the hands of a man who called himself the Governor. In three hours we drove past Boston Commons, Harvard, Longfellow's house, Boston's tallest building, Joseph Kennedy's first house, walked through Old Ironsides, drove under the banner that proclaimed the finish of the Boston Marathon, and heard the Governor ham his way through Longfellow's *Midnight Ride* as we rode over the streets that Paul Revere followed.

"What can you tell your friends you accomplished when you get home?" the Governor asked. I perked up.

"Well, you've been personally escorted by 'the Governor.' You've crossed the finish line of the Boston Marathon..." The Governor paused as though he couldn't exactly remember what to say next, then spoke into his clip on mike. "Oh, yes," the Governor added, "You've 'gone to Harvard.'"

Back home, I thought of other accomplishments. I learned we could not drive from Chelmsford to Braintree, by way of Concord and Boston, as simply as we negotiated New Glasgow to Tracadie, by way of Merigomish and Malignant Cove.

I expected enthusiastic students scampering among the trees at Walden Pond, curiosity shining in their youthful faces.

"Gosh, Dr. Milner. We had no idea that American literature was such a rich and complicated field. What a great opportunity it has been, going to the actual place where great literature was written!"

I've taught English 444 once every three years or so. Lately, I"ve had lively and enthusiastic classes. Most years I had too many students to take to Boston.

I began the field trip as Mr. Chips, and returned as Captain Ahab, brooding alone over a personal obsession. My posture demands I blame the students for the failure of the trip and the course it was part of. In truth, it was my fault.

Hiking in the woods is not necessarily an English major's pleasure. It is my pleasure, learned from Thoreau and from my outdoorsman father, and from the almost unique fate of being a literature professor in a town that doesn't have a metropolis within eight hundred miles in any direction. Where others have operas, and movie houses, and the ballet, I have hummingbirds and trees. I have no right, I realized, to force my choices on students as part of their literary education. English majors tend to favour libraries, artificial light, rooms with nice furniture.

The trip failed because I had changed for the worse. I receive letters from former students. They remember an energetic prof who organized poetry readings, started a club for English students, a friendly guy who drank beer with them at the Golden X, but talked as though Hawthorne and Thoreau were important. That young professor — idealistic in his assumptions, evangelistic in technique, American in bark and whistle — like the Golden X where he performed part of his ministry, is gone.

He's been replaced by a self-absorbed half-century old professor with hairs growing from his ears and a short attention span where other people's games are concerned.

I had no more right to insist students go wandering in the woods when studying Thoreau, than I would to insist they conceive an out-of-wedlock child when they study *The Scarlet Letter* (though an unwed parent would understand some things that most students miss in the book), or to run away from home when they study *Huckleberry Finn*.

Students of literature study texts. It was not my right to make them live like Thoreau. I had been sharing Thoreau's insights as though the insights were in themselves beautiful poems. I'd been doing the intellectual equivalent of a forced march. I should have simply made Walden Pond available. That is what Thoreau would have done. I tried to be a leader, a good guy, a dignified professor, an evangelist for the power of outdoor nature. No wonder my students were catching colds.

Worse, I had placed my single serious student in a crossfire between my Transcendentalism and the general desire of her classmates to see Fenway Park, gift shops, the place they sell Boston Bruins clothing, the original Cheers tavern.

I have something to teach. The readings are particularly difficult; students who are not stirred by them usually find them boring. The course isn't for everyone.

Every year I invite my students to my home in October. We go down to the river, perhaps crush and press some apples. I ask them to write about what they see. They write that they love nature, because they think I want them to write that. When I read these passionate testimonials, I am struck by the fact they most of them saw almost nothing.

Living with intensity in outdoor nature sounds silly to those who don't do it. Most people can't do it, and those who do respond to outdoor nature do it with or without reading Thoreau. They read Thoreau and find replication of what they have discovered on their own. The weight of student ennui, bureaucratic rigamarole, departmental politics, the distractions in my own life, and the widening gap of years between the students and me, made it simpler to be less.

We hardly talked at all on the trip back home. My best student coughed and coughed. Ernest bought a tape of James Taylor's greatest hits, so we played it over and over on the 800 mile trip home. *Fire and Rain* and my best student's cough, over and over, through the empty state of Maine, across New Brunswick, to Antigonish, 800 miles of fire and rain and coughing.

> I've seen fire and I've seen rain
> I've seen sunny days
> that I thought would never end.
> I've seen lonely times
> when I could not find a friend.

That cough would echo around our seminar room like a guilty conscience until April, every Monday and Wednesday evening from five until six fifteen. In April, when she went home, she took that cough with her, but it lived in my memory, a metaphor for the kind of teacher I had to stop being.

My life wasn't working. I was a teacher who didn't believe the words that were coming out of his mouth. Worse, I moved in a world that was eager to swallow my pretentions. The Dean, the students, the citizens of Antigonish, all felt a little happier if I postured as a brilliant intellectual. I was hooked up, with noisy desperation, to a sprawling farmhouse with rotten windows, no insulation, and a mortgage worthy of Mark Twain himself. And Thoreau insists in *Walden* that people do not have to lead meaningless and unhappy lives, that it is possible to live spontaneous and joyous lives in nature. Thoreau promised to be my guide out of a life that wasn't working.

Every day, especially in February, I escaped to the woods. I did not see my students or my English Department colleagues there. I saw a professor of mathematics, a professor of sociology, a professor of biology, sometimes. They were out there because they knew (without reading Thoreau) what Thoreau knew. I also saw Mr. Oostvogel, who farms the acreage across the river. He was ploughing, clearing, or looking after his Holsteins. I saw kids, my own kids and kids they knew. They were trying the ice, climbing trees, fishing, and skipping stones, working on a ramshackle cabin they were trying to build. In the summer they'd be eating berries and apples, floating rafts. Ike-san was always there, sometimes coming upon me for a chat, offering me a nip on his rum. His head was bare, winter and summer. He'd tell me about the clouds, the water level, the fish and deer. I suspected he was amazed at what I didn't know. Sometimes I knew he was watching me and not making himself known.

"There is no one there except me and the river and the sky and the trout. I couldn't own that river and those fish any better if I had a title to it," the mathematician told me. When he described the movements, the cunning, the habits of the fish, his eyes would light from inside.

There is sympathy in the way the hunter stalks the rabbit or deer, though Thoreau doesn't do it. "I have found repeatedly, of late years, that I cannot fish without falling a little in self-respect. I have tried it again and again. I have skill at it, and like many of my fellows, a certain instinct for it, which revives from time to time, but always when I have done I feel that I would have been better if I had not fished...There is unquestionably this instinct in me which belongs to the lower orders of creation; yet with every year I am less a fisherman, though without more humanity or even wisdom; at present I am no fisherman at all."

Thoreau boasted that you could hypnotize him, and drop him in the woods any time of the year, and he'd tell you the date, within two days, by looking at the birds, flowers, quality of light, snow or rain, and the trees and insects. When I first came to Antigonish, I was impressed by that paragraph. But three years of walking and looking back there, and I can almost do it myself.

Ike-san can certainly do it. He can do it is well as Thoreau. In summer he crosses the West River in his homemade boat, and he goes to the shack he built on top of the hill on the other side. In February and March he walks across on the ice. He eats the fish he catches there, the deer he shoots there, the raspberries and black berries he finds there. He heats his house with the wood he cuts there. He has done this for sixty years. He tells what the weather is going to be tomorrow from the clouds, the direction of the wind, the quality of the light.

I have a student who took Thoreau's advice. Instead of living with the students in residence or off campus, he found an abandoned shack, overlooking the Atlantic, just off the Harbour Road. He lived alone. But he saw bending brown grass, the Atlantic ocean in all its moods and seasons. He knew where his heat came from, because he carried the wood, and lit the fires in his woodstove. I took two students to his shack on a windy day, the ground covered with snow, the sun shining.

"I want to teach after I graduate," he said. "I can continue this life, wherever I go. I plan to teach."

"Thoreau was a teacher for a while," I said.

"I'll find a shack like this one, hitchhike back and forth," he said.

"That's where Henry ran into trouble," I said. "People don't like to think the teacher of their kids is strange. Henry and his brother had a school, and it folded. "Teachers don't live in shacks. They buy houses, make mortgage payments. Teachers don't hitchhike. They drive cars."

"Do you believe that?" he asked.

"I don't think any school board I know would want a teacher hitchhiking back and forth," I said. "The parents will gossip about you when they see you standing by the road. The school board will tell you to shape up. That's what I think would happen."

He didn't believe me. And, perhaps, this student will be strong enough to live his life on his own terms. Thoreau was, but he didn't last as a school teacher.

Thoreau wrote about Concord, Massachusetts, and the people there, and the woods a mile and a half outside it. Ralph Waldo Emerson was his friend and champion. Emerson tried to be fair to Thoreau, whom he found perverse. Thoreau resented Emerson, who hired him as a gardener.

Hardly anybody bought his books. Emerson helped him get a few things accepted by magazines, but nothing was particularly popular in his own day. He quarrelled with Whittier and Lowell; Hawthorne had his doubts. Howells didn't think much of Thoreau either. What they agreed to publish, these official custodians of the American Muse wanted to edit. He wouldn't stand for that.

So he stayed in the woods, in the garden, and he wrote. He harangued the world he knew, Concord, for its stupidity, hypocrisy, dishonesty, and small mindedness. The world smiled behind its hand at him.

Without *Walden*, I would not be speaking of the certainties I speak of in this book. Yet, my life has much Thoreau would disapprove of. He would certainly disapprove of my long flirtation with the tavern and the grape, my hooking myself up — with noisy desperation — to a family, to a huge old house with a mortgage; my inability to survive without the financial and social underpinnings of a university.

The woods near the West River are as wild in 1992 as the woods near Concord were when Thoreau went to them in 1845. You can see, as I do almost every day, an eagle in an elm tree waiting for a floating fish, a deer gliding through a meadow; a field of green grass in June, and blueberries the size of peas in August. This August the river was so shallow that I took to walking in tennis shoes, from MacNeil's to Ikemoto's, a half-hour walk in the water that I could make without getting even my shorts wet. In April, when I canoed it twice, it was over my shoulders, and when I tipped the canoe and was dumped from my boat, it was over my head. The current was so fast that I couldn't fight it. But in August, except where it flows over rocks, you cannot see any current at all.

And you spend your days with fields of blooming wildflowers from May through October, eating the cucumbers you planted yourself, smelling the manure in May, watching a hummingbird sucking on a geranium in July, picking strawberries in July, tomatoes in August.

Thoreau acted like it didn't bother him: "For a long time I was reporter to a journal, of no very wide circulation, whose editor has never yet seen fit to print the bulk of my contributions, and as is too common with writers, I got only my labour for my pains. However, in this case my pains were their own reward." Thoreau's journal was published 60 years after he died.

Fame wouldn't come on the only terms he could accept it. So he continued his slow march to that drum only he heard. He stumbled onto the way he was supposed to live so he could write.

In *A Week on the Concord and Merrimack Rivers*, he says of the eyes of people he meets when he goes to town: "It is wonderful how we get about the streets without being wounded by these delicate and glancing weapons."

He drops this into the middle of a passage about boating on the Concord River. Even on the river, away from the opinions of his neighbours, he remembers insults and slights.

If I stay on the river and in the woods, if I stay out of the faculty bar, the hall way, the coffee lounge, I reach a point where my journal and the life it records don't know or care what Antigonish is saying. My February thoughts settle on the snow — powdery or wet? — the return of the redpolls, the deer leaving tracks on the ice of the frozen West River.

"To a philosopher all *news*, as it is called, is gossip and they who edit and read it are old women over their tea." And a page later: "If we respected only what is inevitable and has a right to be, music and poetry would resound along the streets. When we are unhurried and wise, we perceive that only great and worthy things have any permanent and absolute existence, that petty fears and petty pleasures are but the shadow of the reality."

But this is a hard argument to win with myself. The coin of day-to-day intercourse with my neighbours is opinions about the Contras, the Referendum, Mulroney's standing in the polls, Bush's future, who the new AVP will be, who got promoted, or the Acadia game, whether Fred Doucet got dumped, the ins-and-outs of the New Year's Eve dance, whether we'll get a new waste disposal plant, any thing pitched up by the CBC.

I read and hear of our internationally recognized professor-writers and professor-critics and professor-chemists, and our famous Canadian playwright and poets and music conductors, the famous English professor who lectured on three continents last month, and I think maybe I need a drink or a long walk.

Without the commitment of a lived life behind them, the insights of genius are aphorisms to put on student posters, canned goods. If the learned professor doesn't build a life on the literature he or she teaches, the professor is wasting everyone's time.

Henry David Thoreau called it sincerity at the beginning of *Walden*. "I, on my side, require of every writer, first or last, a simple and sincere account of his own life, and not merely what he has heard of other men's lives; some such account as he would send to his kindred from a distant land." Thoreau considered himself the only sincere man in a town that was about the size of Antigonish.

But he was a celibate bachelor. It didn't matter to him that betrayals cut many ways, that pain is as likely to rain down on the betrayed, the accomplice, and the innocent bystander as on the betrayer. The shadow of a personal betrayal falls over the words of this book. Nathaniel Hawthorne, Thoreau's friend who didn't have to publish his books himself, wrote something that fits my style in this book better. "'Be true! Be true! Be true! Show freely to the world, if not your worst, yet some trait whereby the worst may be inferred,'"

I ski down the road, through Ike-san's gate, past his rotting car hulks, to the West River. The river is frozen. I walk on the ice around the bend, under the salmon wire. The snow is piled so high you cannot see over it. It squeaks under foot. Crow and gull tracks break up the unpatterned whiteness on the river. Mice and rabbit and deer tracks and droppings colour the snow. Lar's worn boot tread along the bank and onto the frozen West River, the rutted track of snow mobiles. And my skis, two white tracks in the white snow.

I lean into the wind, covered against the blowing snow by parka, big mittens, and scarf. Looking out through slits in my hood the size of postcards. I feel the clean bite of a winter that has been too long. I long to be free of woodstoves, ash buckets, woodsmoke, and carting wood through my house. I long to feel a hot sun burn my pallid skin.

I step onto the West River ice, and the eagles abandon the elm trees and fly languidly upriver to the curve where the channels prohibit people from entering except when the river is frozen. The eagles hover fifty feet above, hardly moving, like kites, their crochety white heads curious.

3

"So! You go walk?" Netta-san asked when I came to her gate. She was carrying a bamboo ski pole, which she used as a walking stick. She had been shovelling snow.

"Yeah, cold," I said.

"I wish I have time to do that," she said. "Too much work to do. Wish I was a professor, deshow?"

Usually, I see her at the barn, throwing manure out the window, shovelling feed for her horses, shaking her head at her inability to get more work out of the four full-grown men who lived in her house — Ike-san and his four sons. .

"Want muskrat carcase?" she asked.

"No, I can't think of any use I have for one right now," I said.

"Paul kill ten muskrats every week this time of year."

"The eagles followed me around the bend," I said. "They must have thought I was going to feed them some of your muskrat."

Last month I came upon two dogs gnawing on a dead deer on the ice. I didn't know either of them, though both had collars. One was a whitish brown, and the other looked to be at least partly Labrador. They growled when I approached, barked, then slinked away. A deer dead on the ice, of fright, because her hooves couldn't get the traction to escape the growling and biting dogs. The deer's body was still soft and warm. Its eye was open, brown and soft and unfocused, like a horse-chestnut on a tree. I walked around to Ike-san. He was cutting firewood.

"Lady OK no?" he asked. "Lady?"

If I say, yes, he has to shoot his dog.

"Not Lady," I said. "I didn't know the dogs," I said. "One looked to be part Lab, but it wasn't Silvers'. The other was white or grey. I've never seen them before."

Every day I skied or walked past the dead deer. Each day there was less deer to see. One day his eyes were gone. Legs disappeared, or were strewn on the frozen ice. Then it snowed again, and that was the end of the deer. In the spring thaw, I found a hoof in my yard.

Thoreau liked to give things up, though he was too honest to be sure that his renunciations were all morally virtuous.

He not only gives up fishing and hunting, but tobacco, alcohol, meat, and sex as well. He gives up everything he can give up. Strip life to its essentials. "Nature is hard to overcome, but she must be overcome."

His renunciations help him to "flow toward God." I don't seem to have the power not to drink a dozen glasses of draft at the Triangle, to not overeat, not to go with the moment sometimes. I'd prefer not to think what I might be flowing toward sometimes.

He earned his right to gloat. "I see young men, my townsmen, whose misfortune it is to have inherited farms, houses, barns, cattle, and farming tools; for these are more easily acquired than got rid of. Better if they had been born in the open pasture and suckled by a wolf, that they might have seen with clearer eyes what field they were called to labour in. Who made them serfs to the soil? Why should they eat their sixty acres, when man is condemned to eat only his peck of dirt? Why should they begin digging their graves as soon as they are born? ...How many a poor immortal soul have I met well nigh crushed and smothered under its load, creeping down the road of life, pushing before it a barn seventy-five feet by forty, its Augean stable never cleansed, and one hundred acres of land, tillage, mowing, pasture, and wood-lot."

It is Puritan simplicity that Thoreau discovered, and made his own. One of his intuitions is that simplicity is tied up with honesty.

"An honest man has hardly need to count more than his ten fingers, or in extreme cases he may add his ten

toes, and lump the rest. Simplicity, simplicity, simplicity!
I say, let your affairs be as two or three, and not a hundred
or a thousand; instead of a million count half a dozen, and
keep your accounts on your thumb nail. In the midst of the
chopping sea of civilized life, such are the clouds and
storms and quicksands and thousand and one items to be
allowed for, that a man has to live, if at all, by dead
reckoning, and he must be a great calculator indeed who
succeeds. Simplify, simplify. Instead of three meals a
day, if it be necessary eat but one; instead of a hundred
dishes, five; and reduce other things in proportion."

But I am committed to a mortgage, a car and
renovation loans, VISA cards, a MASTERCARD, checking
accounts in two banks and a credit union, three kids who
take basketball lessons, ballet lessons, art lessons, and play
on teams that travel, seemingly, any-damned-where in
North America, a son who has just recently stopped
scurrying around on an expensive skateboard.

It was February 28, the first bright and warm
evening of the year. Hard ice, warm air, clear night; it
was a perfect evening, and it might be the last evening of
the year that I would be able to ski on the West River. I
could hear, far away, trucks humming over the bridge on
the Trans-Canada highway.

Edging up the bank, coming off the ice, something
gave, and I was flailing my arms, my legs under water.
Then I got an elbow on solid ice; my head was above
water. The rest of me was in the river. The current
wanted to pull me away and down.

I flailed and got my right foot out and its heavy ski
onto the ice. I flailed some more, but it wouldn't move.

"Help!" I yelled. I felt so calm. I was going to die. I was an eighth of a mile away from my house, a little closer to MacNeils'. There was the slightest mist settling on my face and it felt good. I could see the yellow lights in the family room window of my house. I thought of them watching television and eating popcorn. I was loved. I could see smoke coming up MacNeil's chimney. I was too happy to die.

"Help!" I shouted. "Help! Help!"

It was surprisingly comfortable. The leg on the ice, the soggy boot, the frozen pants leg: nothing was cold. Stars were bright, hardly a hum of wind in the trees across the river, a pale quarter moon to the South above Sherbrook. I spotted the big dipper. If my boot is stuck in the muck, it cannot be over my head. I am not going to drown. Hypothermia, maybe. Is that why I'm not cold? Bright stars, no wind, yellow lights in the houses, no wind, a shield of black ice. My hat was still on my head. I took off my mittens, slipped the ski pole straps from my wrists, and set them safely on the hard ice. No false steps. I reached into the water with my right hand, found my ankle, and jerked it. My boot lifted from the muck. I grabbed the tip of the ski with my hand, and guided it out of the water through the hole in the ice. I rolled over carefully. I was lying on solid ice. I felt so cool and lucid.

I squished up the path to my house. I took off my skis, set them on the veranda, and sneaked up the steps. I changed into long underwear, wool socks, wrapped myself in a comforter. I went downstairs to tell my tale.

4

Netta-san knocked on the door. She held a huge manilla envelope. Her car was parked in front. Her big dog, Jennie, had followed her up the lane.

"I said I show you picture of your house, and you not believe me, deshow. Well, here is, deshow."

She handed me the manila envelope.

"Jennie's not feeling good. Her pups sharp teeth, hurt tits," she said. "Poor thing. No nothing to be done, wakaru?"

It was an amazing picture, an architect's drawing of my house, with carefully tinted green trees and bushes, a white house, and these long low rows of chicken houses that must have existed once. It was at least fifty years old.

"Chicken coops," she said. "Those chicken coops, yeah. Cunninghams had 50,000 chickens when this picture was made."

"These are nice, Netta-san," I said. "It's nice of you to let me see them."

An old brass bed sat on our veranda. We'd had found it in the attic of our shed. We planned to clean it up, re-paint it.

"So! Where that come from? I have bed just like that, so only it have round hinges. From my mother. My mother, and the master, and Ike-san's father, we all live together, in same house. That's how my mother got pregnant with me. She said she just lived there, and pretty soon she going to have a baby. 'You must have been doing something,' I say. 'It take man to help make a baby,' I tell her. 'Sex!' she said. 'Always sex. I hate sex.'"

"Does Ike-san bother you when you cut wood? I tell him, 'you leave Mr. Milner alone. He cut wood the way he wants to. It keeps him out of trouble. That's why he does it. He don't want you nose in there, tell him how to sharpen his saw'."

"Ike-san is ok in my book," I said, but I don't think she was listening. She pulled the picture and manila folder from my hand, and headed down the steps toward her car. She opened the door to her Volvo, and shouted up at me.

"You send him home if he bothers you. He just sit in that old car — drinking all time. That all he do. He a drunk when he 14 years old. Imagine! I just come to Canada from Shinjuku, the very first week. Where Ike-san? I asked. I asked everyone. Where Ike-san? So! Then they found Ike-san up in the hay mow, drunk as skunk. Imagine!" I smiled. "You no believe me, but it true. Drunk as skunk up in barn, deshow. He no help it, deshow. He try drink himself to death. He told me once, he go to shoot me, and then shoot himself. I no believe that. But he want to drink himself to death. Don't give him any rum. Good-bye."

She walked out to her ancient silver Volvo, opened the door, sank onto the seat, and rumbled up the lane towards the stop light and Sobeys.

Spring
The Professor Lectures on Lobster

Beginning May first when the season opens, and lasting a couple of weeks after that, we eat lobster. It took a trip to the Mira River to put me onto this fine Maritime springtime ritual. I would be a derelict guide, Patient Reader, if I did not share what I have learned.

Hooray, Hooray, for the first of May.
Antigonish Lobster season begins today.[1]

I ate lobster for the first time in my life at a dinner party during my first year in Antigonish. I'd lived ten years in Antigonish without learning to love eating lobster. My lobster was served up with a green salad, a pasta dish, rolls and butter, and dessert after. It was good; but somehow I had expected more. Later, I had lobster in Antigonish's most famous restaurant, the Lobster Treat. Good again, but the shell was hard; the meat was tough.

I wondered what the fuss was all about. Then, one soft summer night after my third year here, a former

---

[1]Nice, but there is something nicer about the American midwestern original: "Hooray, Hooray, for the first of May./ Outdoor sex begins today."

student invited my wife and me to his cottage on the Mira River.

When you go to a lobster feed on the Mira, you go to eat lobster: no rolls and butter, no thoughtfully chosen side dishes. No knives, forks, spoons, lobster shears, or nutcrackers either. What there is, is first, men in ball caps. They run back and forth from the boiling pot, and shout manic instructions at their wives. The wives are stationed at a picnic table where they can admire the cuisine and compliment the chefs. On the Mira, men cook; women witness.

The picnic table is covered with copies of the *Cape Breton Post*, which serve as a tablecloth. In the centre there is a saucepan of melted butter, and a platter bulging with steaming lobsters; a bottle of Schooner Beer sits beside each plate. Off to the side an inverted propane torch heats the lobster pot.

Here, I must digress to tell you something that Maritime women keep from their husbands. *Anyone* can cook lobster well. If you follow this simple recipe, your lobster will be as well-cooked as anyone else's: fill a big pot half full of salt water (everyone agrees that the perfect salt water is ocean water). Once the water is boiling, drop the live lobster into the pot. Grab a lobster by the feeler every once in a while, and give the feeler a yank. When you are holding a feeler without a lobster attached, the lobster is cooked. The mystique of lobster has nothing to do with recipes.

While anyone can cook a lobster well, nobody except an expert can eat one properly. The art of the Mira lobster feed lies in the eating, not the cooking, of the lobster.

First, you twist off the tail. Then, taking hold of the sides of the tail from behind, you place your thumbs against the shell on the back of tail, and push the thumbs down while you pull the front apart with your hands. It is not quite as hard to do as to describe, and if you do it right, the meat separates neatly from the shell. Then, you do something that is most impressive to those who have never seen it done. You tear off a claw, place it on the table — sharp side down — lay the palm of your left hand on top of the claw, and smash the top of your hand with your right fist. If you have done this properly, you have opened the claw, and may proceed to eat the meat. But this can be tricky. I have seen beer, shells, and butter go flying. Picnic tables, steady as they are, have shaken. If you hit the claw too hard, you embed smashed shell into the meat and the back of your hand will sting. A good time to sip your Schooner is when someone else is smashing his lobster claw.

After you have finished the claws and the tail in this dramatic and satisfying way, you are ready to do the things that separate the Maritimer from the rest of us. You must have been born here to have the patience and the stomach to eat the legs, the tomalley (green stuff that looks as if its been eaten before), and the roe (called "the red stuff" it tastes like crayons).

The non-Miran sits at his table, his four lobster bodies beside his plate bearing witness to his heroic eating. He wants no more lobster.

"How's she coming, B'y?" the Miran asks.

"Just fine."

"Good, eh?"

"Great," the non-Miran answers.

"What you...you, uh, what you going to do with those?" the Miran finally asks, nodding toward the pile of bodies that sit — claws and tails removed, but otherwise shamefully untouched — in front of the non-Miran.

"Would you like them?" the non-Miran asks.

"You know, I might just pick at them a little," the Miran says.

If he gets the bodies at 9:30 p.m., he will still be picking at them at midnight. The lobster's eight legs are long and thinner than straws, but there is meat in them. The Miran rips off a leg, sucks, bites, squeezes, and chews. Eight times. Then he turns to the green innards. The tomalley is not, contrary to what the non-Maritimer is told at a certain point in every lobster feed, the best part. When I eat the tomalley, I tell myself that soon this moment will be over and I will have passed another of life's small tests.

One topic of conversation at a lobster feed on the Mira is how to tell a male from a female lobster. There are two ways. If you take a male lobster and place it on the table beside a female lobster, you discover that the female lobster has a broader tail. The other way is hard to explain but easy to demonstrate if you have a lobster in your hands. You pick up the lobster, and turn it over so you can see the stomach. You will see a half dozen or so double finger-like protrusions. The upper most protrusions are the genitals. If you flick them with your fingers, you will discover that on some lobsters they are hard and on others they are soft. If they are hard, the lobster is a male.

After such knowledge, what forgiveness?

6

Catholic

Buy another candle, son,
Before you start to pray,
But don't forget to cross yourself
Before you walk away.

— *Stan Rogers*

Why is this happening in March? Why are the windows rattling, the wind whistling inside the woodstove? Why is the snow blowing as though it were January? Every year I am surprised by the weather. It's nastiness feels personal.

Somebody told me the causeway changed everything, made it so the ice wouldn't melt or float out to sea, and that's why March is so bleak. There are just enough nice days to let us know it doesn't have to be nasty. We expect sunshine, warm days, crocuses, the promise of lilacs.

When anyone gets out of a chair at our house, they check the woodstove. As often as not, they drop another chunk or two of wood into the stove.

Last October eight cords of stove lengths seemed like it would be more than enough to get through the winter. But four days ago, the wood on the back porch was gone, the reserve pile beside the patio door was down to a few sticks, and what was left of the big pile across the road was buried under the snow. Once I found it, I had to bend and dig and whack to get it out. I filled the chainsaw with gas for the first time in six months. The kids, seeing what was coming, took off.

It was late March, and there was no help, and I was working in a blizzard, so I heaped it on the edge of the road, where I wouldn't have so far to carry it. I should have piled it outside. I should have carried it in.

My wife pushed Jiggs outdoors to keep me company. Jiggs sniffed the air, yawned, took a leak on one of the cedars, and watched me with interest until my back was turned. Then he sneaked around to the patio door. When I finally went inside, he was asleep beside the woodstove. I'd blocked and split nearly two cords. That should see us through. Cutting wood in March, when you're feeling sorry for yourself, is lonely work. That evening the plough came through for the first time in a week and a half, and Monday morning my wood was somewhere in the snow bank. I dug some out, loaded it onto the cart, pushed it through the drifts, piled some on the back porch and some on the deck outside the patio door.

The now brownish-yellow Christmas tree, which we'd tied to the edge of the patio after Christmas so we could put bird seed on it, shook in the wind, needles blowing off with every gust. It'd been listing to the left for a month. We poured a lot of seed on it, attracting, lately, mostly a lot of quarrelsome jays. They chase off the chickadees and juncos. They're afraid of nothing except the occasionally invading grosbeaks.

At St. F.X., too, the students are snarly, classrooms full of jays and crows, few songbirds. Students' faces are pale or pasty from late hours, sun deprivation, and the student diet of pizza, potato chips, and diet cola. You realize how bad we all look when you see those back from Florida (three bus loads of St. F.X. students) after spring break. They look radiant, glowing with good health. Everyone else looks sick.

The calendar says its spring. We have seen the odd spring day. So, why is the temperature minus eighteen, and why does the wind cut through you like a knife, and why is there still snow on the ground and in the air? Where are the robins, the crocuses?

I'm tired of cold, tired of snow, tired of the wind, tired of woodstoves and ashes, burns on my hands, tired of having a sore back, tired of nagging my kids to close doors, carry wood, tired of this worn out maroon parka that wasn't mine to start with, tired of wood blocks filling my trunk, salt on the road, dumb jokes about what happened to global warming. Three days of plus twelve would cure this hacking cough. This is, I know, my last self-pitying whine of winter. I can almost see in my mind's eye the moist dirt in the garden, my canoe floating under the dying elms on the West River, smell the lilac trees, hear the neighbours who these past five months I've been waving at through scraped-off car windows. But what I see with my eyes open is piles of snow, bare trees, a dead Christmas tree, a crippled dog that won't leave its spot beside the woodstove.

2

And, of course, I'm not drinking. Soon enough I will remedy that.

Shortly after noon on Easter Sunday, I will pull a bottle of Alexander Keith's from the fridge, sit down in the recliner across from the patio door, and drink my first beer in more than a month.

I gave up beer for Lent. Again. How well it has worked! My occasional sore back stops being so sore because the hanging gut that strains it has almost disappeared. I come as close as I can to looking like a million dollars. Some years I become almost thin. I wake up earlier and with a clearer head.

I will be wearing one of the reasonably fashionable pairs of pants I picked up for a song at the Clothes Mill the last time I weighed less than 180 pounds. My side of the closet is a third full of these great pants. They don't wear out because they only fit for the week or so before Easter, and the month or so after.

I do it for God, for my religion, for the Church. I make this sacrifice for my faith. But, lately, in the new Church, I've been told God might not be so interested in my little sacrifice. Where is the passion of Christ in all this? the new Church asks. Where is the faith that asks me to turn the other cheek, to love my enemy, to help the meek, to comfort the lonely? God, or His earthly representative in my life, the Church, now suggests (very politely; I asked a priest and a lay teacher, and they didn't really want to tell me this, though they seemed to believe it) that I might be missing the point.

Why don't I, for Lent, one of them finally suggested, truly listen to my kids, be quietly nicer to my excitable neighbour who goes crazy when I let the dog out at night to bark at the moon?

The trouble with that kind of sacrifice is that at the end of the day, I don't know if I've done it or not.

Following Father's advice, I vowed to listen to my kids. But my kids didn't vow to talk to me. In fact, as I stood by the door, a model of parental openness, prepared to smile and listen and make helpful suggestions, I almost got run over as the youngest, car keys in hand, headed for the door. And, though I was a bit short with my wife, who could blame me? She asked me to turn the radio down while I was nobly and selflessly emptying the dishwasher for her.

It's hard to know if I'm succeeding with these truer sacrifices. They feel like business as usual. Show me a magazine article about how to be better, more open, more caring, with a ten-step program for success, and I'll probably give it a try. Sad to say, the new Lent doesn't feel like Lent at all. No bite, no 40 days and 40 nights of self-denial.

I've pulled a lot of stunts in the past year. I have failed God in large and small ways, and I have failed some people that I love, too. This pain is mine, and I have it coming. I don't want aspirin. I don't want relief.

I'm truly sorry to hear that God might not be pleased, might not care that I am off the golden bubbly, because about that, I truly know. I succeeded. I did it. Forty plus days without alcohol, from Ash Wednesday until Good Friday and Easter. I resisted all temptation to have a beer.

At the end of each day, tired, a mild pain in my lower back that I knew would go away if I capped a bottle of Keiths, an unspent ten dollar bill still in my billfold, a little sadness starting to creep in at the edge of my mind that I know would lift if I capped a Keiths, I knew I honoured that part of my Lenten sacrifice.

Lent seems to be the only time I *can* do it. Actually, the Church apparently says its ok for me to do what I do, to give up the booze. Good discipline, harmless at worst.

Still, I only have to think about it for a moment to know the new church is right. I do it for me. I do it to get my belt above my navel again. I do it because I like the way I look when I'm thinner, bask in the compliments from friends, feel superior to those who can't or don't give up the booze. I quietly glow as I sip my water while those around me are having a cold one and 150 empty calories.

And Holy Week: the Good Friday service which always seems to be on a wet and cold and grey Friday, the lovely Easter mass at Bethany, then to wake up on a sunny Easter Sunday morning, smell the ham and turkey, look at my beer sitting there under the cold meat tray, think of the new leaner and better focused me that has already begun to emerge. No more stopping by the liquor commission for six on the way home, no more chubby guy, no more solitary trips to the Triangle or Library Lounge.

Forty days and forty nights and then some. At the end, it is spring or what passes for spring in Antigonish. Christ is risen from the dead, the earth is re-born, and I come as close to re-birth as I seem capable of coming any more.

3

I am not even sure that I am Catholic. Not sure I'm a real Catholic, anyway. My story does me little credit, and the Church, being the Church, won't like it. But it is experience, and it counts. It sounds so ancient. Converting to Roman Catholicism. Going over to Rome, as the over-heated rhetoric of the 60's had it. Could anyone younger than 40 understand, or even care, how powerful and confident the Church was before it began leaking priests, and its teachings on birth-control, celibacy, homosexuality, and the role of women began to feel like ancient freight?

In 1964 I was 21 and in love with a Catholic. Against a backdrop of politely expressed misgivings ("Mixed marriages have one strike against them," everyone agreed.), we decided to marry. I grew up in a mildly Presbyterian household that was fuzzy on matters of faith, but certain that it wanted no part of the incense-burning, statue-worshipping Roman Church on the wrong side of Centre Street.

I can date my serious interest in Roman Catholicism to July of 1964, when I began, as a condition of marriage, to take the Marriage Instructions. I learned that my wife-to-be and I would be expected to try to conceive children, and that I, as a condition of marriage, had to agree to raise those unborn children Catholic.

I became a Catholic because I wanted to share the religion of the people I was sharing everything else with. No better reason. Weekly, before my eyes, wine became Christ's blood at the altar, and the white wafer placed on the end of my tongue, tasteless but for the faint suggestion of soap from the priest's hand, was His Body.

I didn't feel secure in my complicated faith, and a phrase I kept hearing did not reassure me.

"Converts are the best Catholics."

I heard it from priests, from nuns, from my plumber who saw me at mass. I heard it in late-night conversations, over beer, with university colleagues and friends. I heard it in Indiana where I was born, in North Dakota where I lived for a while, and again in Canada where I have settled for life.

They said it as they said "nice day" when the sun was shining, or, "Fine, thank you," when you asked them how they were. Though it didn't seem to come from the depth of anyone's soul, Catholics obviously enjoyed saying it to me.

I say I wondered if I was a Catholic at all. I did wonder, but now, twenty years after I converted, I confront a different Church. Nobody seems comfortable with it. I suspect I'm as much at home as anyone of my generation.

Hymns from the top 40, guitar instead of organ. Misdeeds instead of sins, a kiss of peace that among the more enthusiastic believers, actually becomes physical. Lay people distribute most of the communion, and do the less sacred reading of the holy word. Lay people, in fact, do most everything except have a real say in matters of faith.

Father Mosquinski is long gone. He's been replaced, at the university chapels I now frequent, by nice guys called Father Brian and Father John. They offer gentle words of comfort over the agony of exams, the heartbreak of Saturday night alone, while an abstract St.

Francis Xavier, who seems to have three eyes, glares every which way from the side of the altar.

It is a new Church that nobody seems to like much, but we should not laugh at it. It is a Church that is bravely trying to renew itself while it waits for the Spirit to show it how.

Meanwhile, the body of Christ still melts on my tongue every Sunday morning, as it has these past twenty years. I have tasted that wafer when I was so full of my own accomplishments that the drama of man's failure to be worthy of Christ's love was lost on me. I have received communion when I carried the hot burden of secret betrayal up the aisle with me, and wondered seriously if the voice of God might shout me from the Church.

I cannot recall a moment in my twenty years when I began to believe in the Roman Catholic Church. Nonetheless, one day I realized it had been some time since I had been pretending. Unlike my born-Catholic colleagues, I don't have the excuse of early training.

I am never sure — though I try not to think about it — about the parting of the Red Sea, the loaves and the fishes, or the heaven that the Church promised. And I still smile, if I let myself, over the Virgin Birth and the Church's insistence that it be an article of faith. But I now see these as the Church's worry, not mine. If my soul depended on me telling you the truth, I would be forced to confess that when I die, I suspect my immortality will consist of my participation in the nitrogen cycle. I will become rain and dirt. Anything more will be a happy plus.

But there is more.

Beyond that, I came to depend upon the deep quietness of St. Ninian's Cathedral as a place to go and think and make the forms of prayer. I like the way the weekly re-enactment of the Last Supper has etched itself in my mind in the years my children have moved from toddlers to adults. I find a serenity on Sundays, sitting in my pew beneath the fifth station of the cross, surrounded by people I know better than I know any other people anywhere. I believe in the suffering of Christ and of my neighbours, believe in the transubstantiation of the communion wafer, believe in all that two thousand years of history have claimed for the Church.

"There is no God and Mary is his Mother," Santayana said. I know what the words mean. I come to the Church for peace on earth, for love, and for forgiveness. If I am to be "saved," in any sense of that complicated word, it will be here, among these alien people, in a Church I came to for the worst of reasons.

But before it can save me, the Church must be saved from itself. Being custodian of the eucharist is not enough, not in 1992. Ideas are my business, and right now the church doesn't want to hear any that it wasn't hearing twenty years ago. Students listen, then speak with their feet. Nobody wants to be a priest any more; nobody wants to be a sister. Pre-marital sex, birth control, abortion, the role of women, new forms of marriage and commitment:

debates rage, but the church refuses to participate. Shaw said "Catholic university" is a contradiction in terms.

In a column in the *Antigonish Casket* the Very Reverend Colin Campbell, Bishop of Antigonish, published what he called a "commercial" for priestly vocations. He explained why he was not including nuns in his commercial. "Priests, after all, are absolutely necessary for the future of the Church, if we are to remain a Eucharistic community. Sisters are a form of Christian life that served for many years, but are not an absolute necessity to the Catholic community."

Surely, a bishop, even in a rural diocese in the Maritimes, cannot get away with a statement such as that. I waited for the public outcry.

But nobody cried out, not the slighted nuns of our diocese, nor the political commentators who make it their business to challenge the complacent assumptions of our politicians, nor my fellow Catholic parishioners; nor even the ever vigilant local feminists.

"It's hopeless," a feminist student of mine told me when I asked her about it. "Fighting the Church is like battling a deaf giant patriarch."

We Catholics have been schooled in obedience. Young Catholics drift away from the Church for its irrelevance long before they challenge it to be more Christian. Young priests (almost a contradiction in terms in the last decade of the twentieth century) know better, but they don't think they can do anything. A few Church leaders think they are obeying a higher law. But most North American priests don't believe that.

I wrote the Bishop. I said, respectfully, that no thoughtful male could consent to becoming a priest in a

Church that didn't understand the relationship between women and men any better than his statement indicated he and the Church did. I added that I could not recommend any student of mine consider becoming a priest or a nun until the Church seriously addressed its systematic discrimination against women.

I showed my letter to my wife, mailed it off, and waited for the notice of excommunication. But the Bishop was not outraged. By return mail he re-stated his argument, and invited me to keep reading his columns. End of the matter. Today, three years after the bishop's complacent comment and my ineffective letter, the pattern has not changed.

We church-going Roman Catholics participate in a pattern of discrimination against women that is illegal everywhere except in the church. The federal and provincial governments — which rightly insist other Canadian institutions address gender issues in hiring, promotion, and pay equity — say nothing to the Church, whose discrimination is the most blatant.

Yet, the Church is powerless to heal itself. Unlike their male parishioners, Church leaders do not deal with wives and daughters. Catholic lay people know things that priests, struck with a vow that cuts them off from some of life's deepest rhythms, cannot know. In the Antigonish diocese, three priests (as I write) are awaiting trial for sexually abusing young boys, charges that have depressing implications when we let ourselves think about them. Mt. Cashel is a grim reminder of the price we pay for our inability to face gender issues.

The Church leadership is so powerful, and its claims go so far beyond mere fairness that nobody wants to take it on. Young Catholics go to mass and fade. Or, sadder, simply fade. Fewer communicants for our dwindling core of aging priests to deal with. Easier to keep the lid on.

Church leaders don't care what I say to them, so long as I don't give anyone else ideas. But giving people ideas is my business. It is time for Church leaders to be as embarrassed as their thinking parishioners are by what is going on in the name of our faith.

There are laws in Canada about what males in positions of power are allowed and not allowed to do. What Church leaders are doing — discriminating against women because of their sex, systematically denying fully-qualified females the right to hold positions of responsibility — is against the law. It is time to start enforcing the laws that everyone else is required to obey.

I will continue to say to my male and female students what most of them already know — that until the Church opens the priesthood to women, lets them hear confessions, preside over the Eucharist, and makes it at least theoretically possible to have a woman bishop or pope — that a Church vocation is not something for an educated Catholic to consider.

In the long run, the problem will solve itself. In a Church in which priests are becoming fewer and older, lay people are taking over more and more of the leadership of the Church. Does anyone think for a second that lay people in the late twentieth century, are going to go along with the exclusion of our sisters, wives, children in this single area of our life? By then another generation of Catholics will have concluded that the Church is irrelevant to their spiritual needs.

And it is so pointless. Our faith is not about who gets to administer the Eucharist, who gets to hear confession. The theological thinking for ending discrimination against women has been done. Some brave Catholic priest-theologians (among others) have risked their careers to do the Church's thinking and to disseminate the results of that thinking. It is time for Church leaders to let some light in.

For my part, I will continue to participate in the mass, make my Easter confession, and put my envelope in the wire basket. The Church remains the official custodian of much of what I know of truth and beauty. My place in my Catholic community, uncomfortable as it is, is an essential of my life.

I will continue to try to live the Christian life as the Roman Catholic Church teaches it. I will try to help Church leaders see what should be obvious, that maintaining an all male priesthood is not an essential of faith. But it is an essential of faith that we love our sisters in Christ. I owe it to the Church to remind the male church leaders of what this means in 1993. As a Christian, I owe it to the women in my life. As a man, I owe it to myself.

Summer

Farewell to a Priest

Sunny and warm, blue sky, plus thirty degrees, a gentle wind stirring the maples and dying elms. It was the kind of early summer day that makes you think of weddings and new life. But on this summer day, we had the stern task of burying another priest.

Father MacLellan lived his three score and ten years, and a lot more. In our year of burying priests, we came in sorrow and pain to say good-bye to Fathers Kehoe and Gatto and Gardiner. But Father MacLellan, unlike his brother priests, was blessed with a long life. He grew old in honour.

Some people I tend to believe, who knew him and knew St. F.X. history, told me that he was never fully appreciated. He was certainly trusted with all the Xaverian family jewels. Order of Canada, honourary doctorates from X, the University College of Cape Breton, and the University of Western Ontario. I don't know what they could have meant, since he was president of St. F.X. and UCCB (Technically, he was founding principal, when it was known as Little X).

It has been a year of burying priests, and as they pass, nobody replaces them. Those who take their jobs tend to be professionals who know more about their immediate jobs — international development, fund-raising, teaching French, whatever — but much less about the larger contexts of Nova Scotia, St. F.X.'s mission, or what we humans are doing here.

When Kendra MacGillivray played "I am the Bread of Life" on her fiddle during communion, we heard the wind that would soon be blowing over Father MacLellan's grave at Glendale. We saw an eternity of rainy November days with Father MacLellan under his stone, and each of us under ours, soon enough. A churchful of people sat and heard that distinctive Catholic Nova Scotia fiddle, far away expressions on their faces. Soon enough, the fiddle proclaimed, soon enough the wind will be blowing over our graves, too.

I knew Father MacLellan as I knew most of the St. F.X. priests. Respect and affection on my part, mild distrust on his. I worked with him on a project at the Coady once. He was an eminence on that project, I a hired hand. But he was gracious and pleasant. I saw him, for years, almost every day, at the Bloomfield Centre mail room. There are several priests I see there, or on the steps going up to Bloomfield, often. He always spoke, was always friendly, though I don't think he knew exactly who I was.

There's always an interesting story connected with a priest's nickname. "Snooky," said with that mix of affection and derision that people use when the subject isn't in the room. I don't know where the nickname came from, didn't know him well enough to be curious enough to ask.

I want this account in this book because something happened at the end of the funeral that, for me, sums up eastern Nova Scotia, the changing times, the life I glimpse but can never be part of. Something happened that could not have happened any place except here, and probably will not happen here much longer. It was not part of the liturgy, or not quite part of it.

At the end of the mass, Father MacDonell said something like this.

"Father MacLellan's mother, when he was a small boy in Inverness County, taught him a beautiful prayer. It is the same prayer Jesus taught his disciples, the same prayer my own mother taught me when I was growing up in Inverness County. The Our Father. But Father MacLellan's mother taught him the prayer in Gaelic, as my mother taught me the prayer in Gaelic. In honour of Father MacLellan and his mother, I will say the prayer in Gaelic."

Then Father MacDonell began to speak in those stern and dignified cadences that in a quarter of a lifetime living here I have come to recognize but not understand. Father MacDonell didn't invite anyone to join in with him. It was more personal than that. He wanted to say the prayer, because I suppose that for him, the words of the prayer and the memory of Cape Breton he shared with Father MacLellan called for the prayer to be stated.

But this is eastern Nova Scotia, where the men who grew up to become priests all learned the Gaelic at their mother's knees. To my right, across the aisle from where I was sitting, the priests were sitting together in their white vestments. I heard first a solitary voice mumbling the words quietly, a syllable behind Father MacDonell, then another, then another, a murmur of voices, building. They, and the Sisters of St. Martha behind them, reciting quietly, as though involuntarily, the words of the Our

Father in a language the rest of us didn't know. By the end of the prayer, the Chapel quietly reverberated with Gaelic. One could feel their love of the man and priest, their acceptance of where they and we are heading, and of that language that ties them to this place and to that other place across the Atlantic. For these men and women, the Marthas and the Notre Dames and the priests, the blood *is* true, the heart is truly highland, and in their dreams, some of them at least, they truly behold the Hebrides.

7 O Canada

If these sketches should prove the means of deterring one family from sinking their property, and shipwrecking all their hopes, by going to reside in the backwoods of Canada, I shall consider myself amply repaid for revealing the secrets of the prison-house, and feel that I have not toiled and suffered in the wilderness in vain.
— Susanna Moodie, *Roughing It in the Bush*

I spent my first August evening watching the sun set over the Atlantic at the age of 32. The smell of salt water and the cry of a seagull do not touch the nostalgic chord in me that a corn row or a field of swaying wheat does.

A while back, during one of those lulls at a party when the room stops bubbling with conversation, these words came out of a friend's mouth.

"I've lived here for twelve years, am raising my children here. I read at mass, collect for the Canadian Association for Community Living. I'm the father of a hockey player and a highland dancer. Why won't the people of Antigonish accept me?"

My friend's wife appeared, and led him from the room.

"Hey, are those Expos for real?" was the next thing I recall someone saying.

I, too, once wanted to belong in Antigonish. I wished to eradicate the blunt directness that people here define, correctly I suppose, as American. I set out to acquire Maritime diffidence and reticence, personality traits that I admired in my neighbours and colleagues. I wanted to become the sort of person who had lived his life with seagulls, Scottish fiddles, salmon, and Don Messer's Jubilee. I even wrote and saw published short stories with heroes like me, only who didn't make as much noise as I made, and to whom I assigned Maritime personal histories.

I'm not a Maritimer, but sometimes I think my children are. I find them respectful to a fault. My son does not wise off or sneer at foolish adults. My daughters do not cake makeup on their faces. None of my children acts as if they own this, or any other place. These would be distinctive qualities in Indiana. The virtues and quirks I discuss in these pages are, for the most part, my children's virtues and quirks.

But I don't want to see more in all this than is there.

2

When I came here, I was struck by how nice everybody was. Now, I'm nice too. I learned that being nice is a social, not a moral, virtue.

My 50-ish friend in English, who, when drinking, patted women's bums, is gone. So is the Italian-Canadian from Toronto, whose exuberant Catholicism was too overwhelming for our quietly Scottish-Catholic ways. He was in a Jesuit novitiate the last I heard, doing well, he told a mutual friend. He didn't miss us, not for a second.

"Exactly where he belongs," we told each other in the coffee lounge.

And the too visibly sexy French instructor with the tiny waist and individualized breasts beneath her tight sweater, who pulled grinning circles of helpless males, me among them, to her at parties. She's gone to a more prestigious university. So is the Australian professor whose devotion to the work of G. K. Chesterton caused concern among those who felt St. F.X. had exactly the right commitment to that corner of Catholic thought. He went back to Australia.

I used to go, every morning after my first class, sooner if my loneliness needed the balm, to the sixth floor lounge of Nicholson Hall. I'd fill my styrofoam cup with coffee and sit down to a conversation in which the rules were as comforting and formal as a minuet.

We listen politely. We don't call anyone's bluff. We suffer fools gladly. We talk about who pulled a fast one on whom; we do the politics that we learned this morning from the *Chronicle-Herald* or the CBC. We smile our smiles. The smiles work anywhere, but here they are necessary to survival. I'm nice, the smiles say. I'm no threat to anyone. We do who is sick, whose relative died, whose kid is causing pain to his or her parents. We do who bought a new car and who bought a new house, and how they got stung. Assemble ten people who've been here for ten years each, and between them, they know what is wrong with almost every house in the County. We offer scorching analyses of the posturing and equivocations of the university administration. They get money and power, after all; and they are stupider and less sensitive than we are, so why shouldn't we? When we speak of ourselves, we offer a mildly comic litany of dented fenders, kids' report cards, minor illnesses, teaching snafus, conferences we're off to or back from, how we're not going to get the paper completed on time. We don't talk shop unless asked, then we try to deny ourselves the pleasure of puffing up with professorly pride.

Real secrets wend their way to the coffee room by a different route. When a secret makes its debut in the coffee room, its hushed tones cling to it. A canny psychologist will lean over and whisper to you and to you alone, "I saw a friend of yours in Toronto, and guess who he was with?" Or, "Did you hear about the Political Science meeting?" Or, "I went to Parent-Teachers last night, and guess who, as usual, made a jerk of himself." Or, "Guess who is never going to be a full professor so long as Johnny is AVP." Such gossip is juicy, devastating, and always almost true, or better. It contains information you need to hold your place on the pecking order, get grants, save money.

Professor B, the historian, has less interesting secrets. His smiling and hopeful face will cloud for a moment.

"Did you hear the latest?" he will whisper.

We all know Professor B's secrets are as secret as an old newspaper. Still, we plant expressions of mild interest on our faces. He tells his secret.

"Yes, I know," the canny psychologist will say, and he will add a detail Professor B doesn't have.

"Life," someone sighs after a discreet moment.

I have entertained theories advanced by Ph.D.'s in psychology to explain the quirks of personality of my colleagues, as well as the politicians in Ottawa and Antigonish; by Ph.D.'s in engineering to explain why no one should buy a colleague's house with a certain style of insulation; by physical therapists to discuss a colleague's heart attack or bad ankle. I know (or can know if I want) who is having money problems, health problems, whose article was turned down, who lost or got a government grant, who has moved into one of the spare rooms at the Coady Institute, who is having an affair, who is tying himself or herself into knots over what, and who is angry with which of my colleagues.

I learned that gossip is almost always true. Secrets just lie there, in the deep background, waiting to explain a behaviour or a decision when they become relevant. Only a fool would think the gossips do not know everything about him, that in their discussions they don't put the most malign interpretation on what they know. But they are polite. It hardly hurts at all.

Like circus performers we Antigonishers dance on our tightrope in public. When you fall, everybody sees you floundering. Nobody will forget. Nobody will say anything. You become, in your small way, the stuff of legend. Your adventure will be told and retold, when you are not in the room.

Your stock rises and falls according to a rhythm that has only something to do with what you are doing. People who have been cool suddenly become friendly. Former half-friends go a step out of their way not to trade banalities with you. Someone whom you usually don't chat up gives you a big wave from half way across the parking lot, and then invites you to dinner. A colleague with whom you are accustomed to trading weather and ailment reports in front of the mailboxes marches by without seeing you.

These small alterations in the rhythm of your life derive, sometimes, from gossip heard in the coffee room or at one of the thousand parties the hundred and fifty of us give each other each year. We are judged by our niceness, our professional reputation, how much money we have, our competence, our ability as carpenters, story-tellers, gardeners, house-keepers.

When I moved here, people seemed cruel in what they said about each other. People I knew from elsewhere believed that if you couldn't say something nice about someone you shouldn't speak about them (They didn't practice the belief too well, but lip service at least was paid to it). I wasn't used to people saying what they truly felt about those not in the room.

A colleague, whose task it is to make sure that we arrive properly attired for those occasions for which academic gowns are expected — funerals, closing exercises, memorial masses — and who is therefore a frequent protagonist in our ironic stories, told me this, once, as we were puzzling gossip:

"People here forget nothing and learn nothing."[1]

I don't know why it should be so, but gossip doesn't have wisdom in it. There is truth in the Scottish proverb that says that in order to survive small town gossip you must either be a reprobate and not care what people say, or you must live such a blameless life that there is nothing

---

[1] He told me another thing about gossip that I have passed off as my own so many times that people probably think I made it up. "I don't repeat gossip," he said with mock dignity before laying some good stuff on me. "So listen carefully. I'll only say this once."

juicy to tell about you. Most of us do not qualify on either count.

News travels from mouth to ear. You're not supposed to write it down. You can say anything you want about the Bishop, the president of the university, a colleague's research or house, but do not write it down. Maybe, its because we all know the worst about our neighbors, about what is going on on the school board, what the dearly departed was really like, who is dogging it on the English faculty, what the Church is not doing for the spiritual life of its communicants. I used to blame the *Casket* for accepting everything and everyone at their pretensions. But, in small town life, it is part of our politeness. We have to live with each other.

Still, if we can't put our defects down, if we cannot truly face the worst about ourselves, we cannot know our virtues either. If our friends's defects are off limits, and our enemies's virtues cannot exist, we can't know the truth about either our friends or our enemies. We can't truly know who we are.

The truth sets us free, every time. People don't think they want to hear it, but they really do. The charm of the truth grows on people. If they don't like it now, they usually come around to liking it in six months, after they forget the writer said something that should not have been said.

I was trained in the soon-to-be-forgotten art of properly using necessary footnotes. Footnotes give extra information, helping the writer make the point that this book, like life itself is denser and richer and has more layers than the basic text can say. I like to see them in books. It gives them heft, gravity. Footnotes appeared in early novels. Sterne used them to good effect in *Tristram Shandy*; Fielding's *Tom Jones* has them, and, in more recent times, so does James Joyce's *Finnegan's Wake*, and John Fowles' *French Lieutenant's Woman*. Why shouldn't I include them in the *Yankee Professor's Guide*?[2]

I know a dozen people here better than I knew almost anyone outside my family in any other place I have lived. I also know about the triumphs and frustrations, suffering, small and large betrayals of another three hundred people more intimately than people in larger places know anybody they don't choose to know. I am talking about my colleagues and neighbors, of course, but also the milkman who won $25,000 in the lottery, the carpenter whose son had a bone marrow transplant, the lady who came to collect for Recovery House whose husband moved into an unused room at the Coady Institute to dry out before making one last effort to save their life together.

The grapevine also tells me of a colleague coping with cancer, of a colleague bravely (given the pervasiveness of our gossip) handling an out of wedlock grandchild, of a hundred small acts of love and self-denial.

In my seventeen years I have seen people lead lives with nobility and grace. If I live long enough in Antigonish, and if I don't turn sour, or cruel, or alcoholic, I might grow into a wise old man. That can happen when you know everyone else's business.

---

[2]But not everyone agrees.
"Reading a footnote is like having to go downstairs to answer the doorbell when one is upstairs making love."
— Noel Coward.

After a half hour a day, four or five days a week, for eleven years or so, I decided that there was not much more that the coffee room could teach me. Even so, giving it up was as hard as giving up smoking. I missed the insights into things like CFL stability, Fred Doucet's shenanigans, the latest shameless move by our administration. I missed the friendliness too, but I concluded I'd find more real warmth elsewhere.

Why wasn't it working for me anymore? The coffee lounge was a permanently spluttering conversation. The topic was hastily changed, every few seconds, as new bodies dropped into just-vacated chairs. Everything in the lounge was deflected. Everything was at arm's length. Those around the table could only jeer or sneer at or pity a third party. The fools and liars and pullers-of-fast-ones were never in the room when their actions were discussed.

I was reasonably sure my short-comings were at least as interesting to my colleagues as everyone else's were. But by its unwritten rules, it could not discuss my stupidity, culpability, double-dealing, or slipperiness except when I was out of the room. I'd reached a point where being cheated or underestimated by deans and vice presidents wasn't something I had much interest in.

When I realized my own life's path had to begin with a serious confrontation of my own stupidity, culpability, double-dealing, and slipperiness, the coffee room could no longer interest me.

I had other lives to live, and no more time to spare for that one. I dropped out of the coffee lounge, the faculty bar, the serpentine dinner party network. Being in the know got in the way of seeing clearly the life I wanted to see clearly.

What's on my mind is not what's on other people's minds.   I was dropped from the editorial board of the *Antigonish Review* during one of its cleansing purges, couldn't line up enough support to get back on.   The AVP decided to abolish the student writing award that I'd worked on for ten years.   When I protested, he kept right on thumbing through his mail and suggested I try to get it re-instituted after he retires.   My opinion is no longer one that people listen to at faculty meetings.   People tell me they thought I was on sabbatical, they haven't seen me for so long.   When they ask me, "What's new?" I'm stumped. If I tell them, their eyes glaze over.

3

One job I had during my first year at St. F. X. was Friday afternoon ice-fetcher for the faculty bar.   I would stop by Albert Whidden's house in front of his trailer park at Main and Hawthorne.   I'd knock on his door, wait, and soon the wealthiest man in town would appear and accept the seventy-five cents I offered.   Mr. Whidden was short, wore gold-rimmed glasses, and his gray hair was styled in a closely-cropped flat top.   I would wait in his outer office, while he disappeared into what looked like the kitchen, and returned with my bag of ice.   He'd hand me the ice, then he'd look at me over the tops of his glasses.

He told me about the Chisholms, who started with a pickup truck and now operate the multi-national Nova Construction Company and the mall out of Antigonish.

"Milner," he'd say. "Who's your father?" He told me of a mountie named Milner who had three beautiful daughters, was I sure I wasn't related to them? He told me about Creighton Jewkes' father, who came here from Cape Breton, and started the Five-to-a-Dollar. Creighton worked hard, and now he owns houses all over town, and the people of Antigonish think a lot of him. He told me how Father Somers, an Antigonish boy, transformed St. F.X. into the major university that it is today. He told me about the Bekkers and Corstens and Van Tassels, outsiders here just like myself, who had made a spot for themselves in this community.

Sometimes, one bag of ice wasn't enough, and I would return from the faculty bar to Mr. Whidden's house late at night. I'd see the silver glow of his tv set as I knocked on the door. He'd re-appear, dressed as before, and let me in. On these occasions I would be glassy-eyed; and, standing in his heated outer-office, I'd wonder if the beer on my breath was noticeable. Sometimes, on these second trips, instead of telling me about good Antigonishers who did well, Mr. Whidden told me night time tales about other Antigonish men, men who did well for a while, but lost it. He told me about a man who owned the most lucrative chicken farm in Antigonish County, but who reached the point where he'd just sit home and drink. When he died, there was hardly money to bury him. He told me about Pete Poirier's boys, many of them from good families. But now they ride the bottle exchange truck, and spend their evenings at the Triangle Tavern. Mr. Whidden was a kind man, and if there was a lesson for me in the night time stories, it was an oblique one. He told them as illustrative of the quirks of fate.

The next year, a newer faculty member took over my job as ice fetcher, and I lost direct contact with Mr. Whidden.   I noted the steady improvement in his trailer court, campground, apartment rental operation, and business headquarters.   Some of my students rented rooms or house trailers from him.   When I visited them in their well-heated, cleanly painted, temporary houses, they said nice things about Mr. Whidden.   This is almost unique. Most of my students who live off-campus live in poorly insulated and unheatable firetraps, and feel they are being exploited by the landlords.   I also met travelers, who stayed all night in Antigonish at Mr. Whidden's trailer camp, and loved our town.   Once I even drank a beer with his son, quieter than Mr. Whidden, but also projecting a canny purposefulness.

I attended (another fold of my life) Chamber of Commerce meetings for a year.   Mr. Whidden spoke seldom, but when he did, everyone listened and then voted quickly to implement his suggestion.   He persuaded the Chamber to print maps of Antigonish, so he could distribute them to people he met on his annual winter trip to Florida.   The maps were on 8 1/2 x 11 typing paper with black ink.   They showed the trans-Canada, Halifax, the Atlantic Ocean, Toronto and a huge Antigonish.   On the back, there was a list of Antigonish facts and virtues.

Eleven years after my days as ice man, my wife and I realized we would not be leaving Antigonish voluntarily. We invited my mother-in-law to move to town.   She needed to store her furniture while she looked for a place to live.   I recommended Mr. Whidden.   His storage unit turned out to be as good as I knew it would be; a room in a huge red barn; reasonable price; excellent security; no leaks.

When she found an apartment four months later my family took three evenings and helped her move her things. Each night I would go to Mr. Whidden's house, knock on his door, ask for the key to his barn, and wait in the outer office while he fetched it.

He told me about the campaign to raise seven million dollars for a new hospital, about more hardworking and successful Antigonish families. He began to tell me about the growth of the university.

"I know about that," I said.

"*You* do," he said the way people say it here.

"I work there," I said.

"I see...," he said.

"I've lived in Antigonish for eleven years," I said.

"Eleven years," he repeated.

"Eleven years used to seem like a long time to live in one place," I said.

"Imagine!" Mr. Whidden said. "Eleven years!"

He handed me the key to the red barn and the key to the inside storage room. Then, he looked at me and smiled his shy smile.

"I hope you enjoy Antigonish," he said.

I will be quick. Life goes on, but the *Guide* must end.   Another of my chickens has come home to roost. Netta-san, my only neighbour who is more foreign than I am, dropped me like a bad habit.

"You owe me eight thousand dollars," were her last words to me, five months ago. "Wakaru? Wakaru?"

"That's the stupidest thing you ever said to me," I replied. "I demand an apology."

I'm still waiting for the apology.   She's been rumbling up the lane in her ancient silver Volvo with her nose as high in the air as it dare go without risking a wheel to one of the potholes.

When we were still speaking, Netta-san told me stories about all our neighbours, stories I greedily devoured and half or three-quarters believed.

Now my dark legend grows whenever she bumps into someone at Sobey's.

"Good riddance," my neighbours say.   "We don't believe Netta-san's stories anyway. We believe you Phil."

But their eyes twinkle, and I don't know what my neighbors believe. My neighbours's reassurances tell me only that they have heard, that they half believe.

It is about land, of course. In spite of my vigilance, my willingness to smile complacently as my neighbours traced the border, and explained their claim to the disputed lands in our neighbourhood, I was stirred in. I will spend the rest of my days as yet another serious player in the Cunningham Road land war, telling my righteous story to half-doubting auditors, showing them the survey, walking off the border, trying to stamp out this incorrect history of our land, trying to make my neighbors believe I'm not capable of moves as slippery as those Netta-san assigns to me.

5

If I learned in Nova Scotia that I didn't get to be a Maritimer, I learned, when I returned home to Indiana, that I wasn't a Hoosier either. I no longer found Indiana humour as funny, Hoosier informality as appealing, or American directness as candidly honest as I once did. And the racism — which I'd not noticed when I lived there — offended me. [3]   Worse, in the place I grew up, they laughed at my accent. It sounded British to them. They found it absurd that one who had baled hay, drunk

---

[3] I asked one of my hybrid American-Maritime daughters about it. She said that she was at first outraged by the overtness of Indiana racism when she encountered it. Maritime racism is subtler, she said, but just as real. She told me of a friend whose best friend was black. They lived together, dated together, drank together. But the best friend wasn't welcome at his parents' house.

What I know for sure about racism in eastern Nova Scotia is that fewer racist jokes reach my ears here than did in Indiana, that my children and their friends have no tolerance for racist assumptions or racist humour, that I like the way my white and minority students at X relate to each other.

Budweiser, and played linebacker, would come back to town with his shortcomings intact (this is not the place for *that* list, but I will note in passing my rambunctious exuberance when I'm into the grape, my secretiveness when I'm not, my willingness to let you think more highly of me than my actions deserve, my lust, and my unforgiving nature once I correct an overestimation of someone else) but without his plough jockey intonations. I had assumed that my Hoosier accent was still in place, because people in Antigonish knew me by it.

Five years ago, in Truro, on this day, wearing my tasteful blue pin-striped suit, I gulped, and swore fealty to the Queen of Canada. The visible signs argue that Canada was pleased. The lieutenant governor and a dozen Legionnaires shook my hand. The Truro High School band broke into "O Canada." Two hundred kids cheered and waved red and white maple leaf flags. They gave me a flag for my lapel, a red *Gideon New Testament* for my pocket, a four-colour poster with pictures of Canadian trees and Canadian animals, an ID card that defined my new nationality. My wife and children were the only people in the auditorium that I knew. I felt silly.

"Congratulations," my wife said, but the former Soldier of the Quarter was sceptical. Had he just betrayed his country? His country? That was the question. Was I a Canadian? Or, more to the point, was I no longer an American? Educated Americans are more-or-less encouraged to feel that Bush and Reagan and Nixon and their ilk are jerks; that American foreign policy is a sinister joke. It is easy to reject the American government, and to prefer Canada's.

On the cusp of a half-century's life, I shook loose from my colour-coded green and blue disks, my compulsive re-writing of my latest 1,000 word essay, my book of short stories, my outdoor book, my perhaps unpublishable classic, *Craigenputtock, Nova Scotia.*

Tonight, it is July first, twilight, and I am standing on our hill eating the tart red currants I planted a few years back. A northern oriole flits among the apple trees above the spice bed. My wife is sitting on the porch-swing reading a book in the fading light. She raises a friendly hand, she who alone besides me remembers Plymouth High School, me as a quasi-heroic linebacker, the American Army in Japan, Jerry Ringle, figured out how to survive in Antigonish with an American accent, agrees with my assessment of three children who have worth beyond that of other children.

Those almost grown children are at Columbus Field tonight, watching the Canada Day ceremonies. If there is less to nationhood than I once thought, I have discovered at mid-life that a quarter century marriage contains more complicated mysteries than the uninitated can dream of.

By now, the Lieutenant Governor has made his speech to Antigonish's new Canadians. My sister and brother immigrant-citizens will have released their helium-filled maple-leaf balloons. At ten o'clock, on tv, I will see some of my fellow immigrants praise Canada's generosity, beauty, and ice cream to the CBC reporter. It seems to me that the way to assert a Canadian identity is not to shout how proud you are to be Canadian. I left a country where every loyal citizen was expected to thank his or her lucky stars to be an American.

Above the hill that leads to town, I hear a pop, and then a bang. My wife has disappeared from the veranda. When she flips on a light, the picture window fills with yellow light. I am spitting currant seeds, hearing garbled words from the public address system almost a mile away, waiting in the dark.

Suddenly, the bursting Canada Day rockets light the darkening sky. The flashes are red and yellow and blue. They make a momentary and confusing brilliance. Then, it is dark again, and the only light I see is this glowing huge rectangle of yellow light that shines from our picture window.